Word, Wisdom & Worship

WOMANCHURCH CELEBRATES THE SEASONS

Sandra Louise Litzinger

WovenWord Press

Word, Wisdom & Worship: WomanChurch Celebrates the Seasons
Sandra Louise Litzenger
isbn: 09658137-6-2
WovenWord Press
811 Mapleton Avenue
Boulder, Colorado
80304
Copyright © 1999
Scripture excerpts marked with ** are taken from the *New
American Bible with Revised New Testament* Copyright © 1986,
1970 Confraternity of Christian Doctrine, Inc., Washington, DC.
Used with permission. All rights reserved.

Cover design copyright © Traci Schalow
Book design copyright © Vicki McVey

Art Work:Colleen Gallagher, O.P.
The egg shapes and spirals on the cover
and in this volume represent the energy
that flows from the feminine, life-giving,
nourishing womb of WomanChurch.

For Marjorie, Marie, and Megan

Acknowledgments

I wish to acknowledge and thank the many people who have contributed to the formation and completion of these pages. The contents reflect years of study, prayer and reflection with women and men of faith, of various backgrounds, and in varied settings. I owe a special debt of gratitude to each of them, as well as to the Scripture faculty at Catholic Theological Union, where I studied almost two decades ago, who encouraged me then and who continue to inspire me through their writings. I want to thank also my recent colleagues in doctoral study at the Graduate Theological Foundation, particularly Pat Clemens, my reader, and the members of my "viva voce" group who first encouraged me to publish this work. Special thanks to Regina Coll, CSJ, for generously agreeing to read and evaluate this manuscript and for her personal encouragement and support.

Thanks also to my friends and colleagues, Kate Halischak and Elaine Tracy, for their support and editorial suggestions, to my sister, Jeannie Litzinger, my friends, Colleen Gallagher, OP, Joan Supel, OP, Ellen Dunn, OP, Danielle Witt, SSND, Camille Dandurand, and Betty Plank who responded across the miles to my requests for feedback. I extend special gratitude and appreciation to my friend, Eileen Kolman, for her daily encouragement, support and understanding and for her careful reading and helpful suggestions.

Finally, to Colleen Gallagher, OP for her inspiring artistic creations, to my publisher, Sheila Durkin Dierks whose encouragement and support have been outstanding, and to my editor, Mary Cabrini Durkin, OSU whose patient and careful critique and helpful suggestions have brought this work to completion, I am most grateful.

Table of Contents

Preface

From ancient times, the change of seasons has been celebrated in myth and ritual. Nature provides the occasion for
people with a common history, a common faith, a common
hope to reflect together, to remember, and to sanctify the ordinary. In the words of Joseph Campbell, "myths and rites were
means of putting the mind in accord with the body and the
way of life in accord with the way nature dictates" (p.70).

Authentic ritual flows out of everyday activity, out of the
rhythm of our lives. Ritualizing is a way of expressing common meanings and common understandings, a recognition
that there is more to life than can be measured or put into
words. Rituals are an integral part of the human experience,
a way of linking the individual to the community and the
community with a tradition that reaches beyond any particular time and place, an expression of a spiritual reality, of rev-
erence and respect.

Many women today, and a growing number of men, are
keenly aware that the predominant world view, rooted in the
European male experience and reinforced by religious ritual,
does not flow out of their reality. Moreover, institutional ritual which is created, controlled, and implemented by men does
not function for women as a link to the community and to the
tradition. Since it frequently excludes the experience of
women in its language, its selection of stories, its choice of
symbols, and its leadership, women are seeking alternative
opportunities to tell their stories and to create rituals that flow
out of their experience and which have meaning for them.

For some women this situation has led to total separation
from the patriarchal religious traditions. For others, those for
whom this project is undertaken, it means searching for ways
to connect with women and men who share their longing for
an inclusive community whose ritual is, in fact, expressive of
their human experience and of their desire for union with one
another and with God.

What follows is a guide for individual or group study, reflection, and prayer that is based on or flows out of the common lectionary readings for selected seasons and Sundays throughout the liturgical year. It focuses on selections that are appropriate for use by women who find it difficult to relate to many of the readings now used at liturgy and who appreciate the opportunity for an alternate experience which is based on Scripture and is connected in some way to the weekly worship of the larger Christian community. This guide is intended for use by men as well as women, either as preparation for or reflection upon the parish weekly celebration of liturgy. It could also be used in place of the current institutional ritual. Since the life experience of this author is female, Roman Catholic, and North American, it does not claim to be inclusive of other cultures, but it is presented with the hope that future revisions of official lectionaries and sacramentaries might become inclusive of the culture, gender, and life experience of all those for whom the readings and rites are intended.

Introduction

SEASONS OF THE CHRISTIAN YEAR

Some of the oldest rituals of which we have evidence were associated with the obtaining and eating of food. And the most ancient Christian ritual is that of breaking bread and drinking wine. Our liturgical calendar evolved as the early Christians selected one Saturday night and Sunday morning each spring to celebrate the new life of the Risen Christ. The community came together in darkness, keeping vigil until sunrise, when they celebrated Eucharist, proclaiming *ALLELUIA! JESUS IS RISEN!!* Gradually, the celebration was extended to several weeks and brought to completion with a commemoration of the outpouring of the Holy Spirit on the young Church, the feast we recognize as Pentecost.

Later, celebrations at the time of the winter solstice were transformed by Christians to commemorate the manifestation of Christ, the Sun of Justice, to the gentile world. In Rome in the fourth century, December 25 was chosen to celebrate the birth of Christ, and in the Greek world, a new feast, the Epiphany or "showing forth," was commemorated on January 6.

The season of Lent, paralleling the season of rebirth in nature, evolved as a period of initiation for those seeking new life in Baptism at the Easter Vigil and as a time for Christians to reflect on the meaning of their own death and resurrection. Later it became a time of penitential observance in preparation for the feast of Easter.

Gradually, the weeks before Christmas came to be observed as a period of preparation for the coming (advent) of Christ at Christmas. These two seasonal celebrations, of the Incarnation (Advent-Christmas-Epiphany) and of the Death/Resurrection (Lent-Easter-Pentecost), along with a time in between (Ordinary Time) for further reflection on these central Christian mysteries, define our current liturgical calendar. The pages that follow focus on selected feasts from each of these seasons. It is hoped that individuals and communities of faith will find them useful in preparation, in celebration, and in reflection.

Use of This Guide

The material presented in these pages is intended to be a guide, a resource, a starting point for personal or group reflection and prayer. It is hoped that its use will ignite creativity in others who will use what is helpful and discard or replace parts that do not emanate from the life experience or enhance the prayerful reflection of users.

The format is basically the same for each of the feasts and, for a particular season, suggested hymns, responses, and so on, may be repeated from week to week. Meaningful repetition is helpful in ritual when it aids reflection and focus. Use of a similar format for each group gathering can be helpful both to planners and to participants. People who feel uncomfortable when asked to participate in the planning of ritual are often put at ease when they have a format or structure within which to work; reluctant participants are more likely to continue if they know what to expect from week to week. Each group will need to decide whether the planning will become the responsibility of one person or a group. It is hoped that such responsibility will rotate and that planners will be as free as their creativity allows or as structured as they and the group choose to be.

The following comments or suggestions apply to the general format used for each feast. Some of these suggestions were made by previous participants; others have been intended from the beginning by the author.

PREPARATION

Background: This section includes information on the scriptural readings and/or liturgical setting for the particular season or feast. It is intended to be read beforehand by all group participants; it should not be included as part of the prayer service, although it might be read aloud to the group before the actual service begins.

Setting: It is important that someone(s) attend to details of appropriate space, music, symbols, etc. beforehand so that these foster rather than distract from a prayerful atmosphere.

Roles:

1. The prayer leader should be chosen beforehand and be fully prepared to lead; the leader should also feel free to adapt language, discussion topics, and so on. Following the proclamation of the Gospel, the leader is encouraged to share her or his own remarks in lieu of the meditation provided.

2. Readers should be asked (or volunteer) ahead of time, at least before the service begins, so that they have an opportunity to read over their assigned parts.

MUSIC

Where suggested music is traditional or in general use at liturgical functions, no specific reference is given; in some cases, only general themes are provided; in other cases, recommended selections may not be readily available to the group. In all cases, whatever musical talent is available in the group should be used and welcomed both in selection and implementation.

USE OF SCRIPTURE

Most of the Biblical texts found in these pages are free adaptations by the author based on a combination of several English translations: *The Jerusalem Bible; The New American Bible; The Bible* (Revised Standard Version). Wherever a passage is quoted directly and exclusively from a particular edition, it is identified with an asterisk in the text and the source is acknowledged on the Direct Biblical Quotations page (134).

Since the purpose of this book is to offer reflection and simple rituals for devotional use, its concern is not limited to what the text once said to a particular people, but with what and how the same text enriches the lives of women and men in contemporary communities of faith. Where adaptions of Scriptural translations are found, they have been made with care to preserve the meaning of the text in the light of contemporary scholarship and in faithfulness to the heart of the biblical tradition. Most of these changes are made in passages where the language or context is experienced today as exclusive of categories of people (i.e. women) or offensive to groups (i.e. the Jewish people). Choice of words is an important element of the total message and spirit of each section.

Discussion/Reflection

These starters will often need to be adjusted to the circumstances of the local group; participation should always be optional and no one should be uncomfortable (or made to feel uncomfortable) during moments of silence. Unscheduled moments of silence allow for creativity and focus, and they allow time for everyone to formulate thoughts so that the more loquacious members do not dominate the conversation at the expense of the more reticent members.

The Season of Advent

As noted earlier, it was common for ancient peoples to mark the seasons of the year with special ritual. The shortest and darkest days were accompanied by fear: fear of the dark and the cold, fear that the winter food supply would not hold out until spring and fear that the source of heat would not survive. However, these days were accompanied also by hope: hope that the darkness would not finally triumph. Then, when it seemed as if the cold and darkness would surely overpower the diminishing rays of light, hope turned to rejoicing as the sun began to linger a bit longer each evening, warming the earth with promise of new life (cf. Huck, p.181).

Advent is a feast of the earth. In placing our observance of the coming of Christ, Son of God and Light of the World, at the time of the winter solstice, Christians were building upon this celebration of the sun which gives light to the earth. Advent is the time to make ready this earth for the coming of God's Son, for the birth of the light that casts out the darkness of evil in the world and in our hearts. It is a time of reflection, of waiting and longing, a time of hoping and of moving into the womb of darkness from which hope and light are born.

Keeping these themes and symbols of Advent in mind, in the section that follows we enter into the season of Advent in the spirit of our ancestors, with fear and hope, in darkness and light, in longing and expectation . . . and, through the darkness, to rejoicing in the light of new life.

ADVENT READINGS AND REFLECTIONS

A Collage of Readings from the Season of Advent: Cycles A,B,C.

Come, let us go up to the mountain of God, to the house of the God of Jacob (and Rachel and Leah) that God may instruct us in divine ways and that we may walk in God's paths (cf. Isaiah 2:3, Sunday I, Cycle A).

Return for the sake of your servants,
the tribes of your heritage (Isaiah 63:17*, Sunday I, Cycle B).

In those days I will raise up for my people a just shoot (cf. Jeremiah 33:15, Sunday I, Cycle C).

There shall come forth a shoot from the stump of Jesse. And a branch shall grow out of these roots (cf. Isaiah 11:1, Tuesday I).

THEME: Hidden Roots

These readings from Isaiah and Jeremiah set a focus for our Advent reflections. They recall our scriptural roots, those faithful women and men, the Hebrew prophets, the matriarchs and patriarchs who prepared the way for the coming of the Messiah. Who are these ancestors, these roots? In the prologue to Matthew's Gospel, the genealogy begins with familiar ancestors like Abraham (and, by implication, Sarah), Isaac (and Rebekah), Jacob (and Rachel and Leah). It continues with Judah and Tamar, a Canaanite who dressed as a temple prostitute to win the favor of Judah; Salman and Rahab, who assisted Israelite spies in the conquest of the Promised Land and who is praised in the New Testament for her faith and works (Hebrews 11:31; James 2:24,25); Boaz and Ruth, the faithful Moabite, a polytheist, who endeared herself to Boaz; David and the wife of Uriah the Hittite (Bathsheba) whose beauty attracted David; and finally, Joseph and Mary. Of Mary was born Jesus who is called the Messiah (Matthew 1:1-16).

Included in the names of ancestors here are these foremothers: Tamar, Rahab, Ruth, and Bathsheba. All foreigners, they were admired in Jewish tradition as women of influence (here we must refrain from imposing our judgments on another time and culture), and they seem to be included in this genealogy precisely because they are outsiders (non-Jews). Symbolic of the extraordinary ways of God, of the unexpected, of irregularities and surprises, they point to the unconventionality of the Incarnation, but they also symbolize all categories of "outsiders," the excluded who are now included in the family of the Messiah-God. "[For] whoever does the will of God is my brother and sister and mother" (Mark 3:35*). The reign of God is filled with the unexpected!

Who, in our Christian tradition, are the excluded? the unnamed? the underappreciated? Certainly, among those generally excluded, unnamed, and underappreciated in both the Hebrew Scriptures and in the Christian tradition are the women. In the brief period, however, during the public ministry of Jesus and in the earliest Christian communities, women were included as partners with men and named as disciples and ministers, even as leaders of churches. In the Gospels, we see Jesus including women among his followers. In his letters, the apostle Paul speaks of women as his co-workers in ministry. (See, for example, Luke 8:1-3 and Romans 16:1-16.)

During this Advent, along with other Christian women whose experience is seldom, if ever, included in the shaping of ritual and whose voices and experience are not heard in official preaching, let us reread and reinterpret those Scriptures that do include women. Let us find resources for spiritual nourishment in the lectionary readings commonly used in public worship during these weeks of Advent, and where these resources are lacking, let us find related scriptural readings that do speak to our experience. Let us begin with stories of our foremothers Sarah, Rebekah, Leah and Rachel, without whom Matthew's genealogy would be quite different (or nonexistent!). Let us reflect also upon our own mothers and grandmothers, our mentors, our friends. Let us allow our lives to be touched by our biblical foremothers; let us be grateful for the gifts of our mothers and grandmothers, of our mentors and friends.

As the days grow shorter and the nights grow longer, let us embrace our fear of the darkness, of the unexpected, of the outsiders. In the strength of our union with strong women of the past who have shown us the way and with contemporary women who inspire and support us, let us journey through the darkness of our personal advents, through the unknowns and the longings of our lives to the promise of light and life. Let us welcome into our hearts and our homes this Advent those outsiders, those interruptions, those surprises that, like the insertion of foreign women into the genealogy, jolt us into new beginnings and new life.

ADDITIONAL SUGGESTED READINGS

Sarah: Genesis 11:29, 30: Abraham's wife; infertile.

16 - 22: Power of Sarah: a spirited woman, a bold companion, a respected matriarch.

16:1-15: Sarah and Hagar; note God's blessing of Hagar, the outsider, the slave.

17:1-22: Covenant talk; Abraham laughs.

18:1-15: Visitors; Sarah laughs.

21:1-20: Birth of Isaac; note 21:12.

Rebekah: Genesis 24-26: Strong, daring, and bold.

Leah and Rachel: Genesis 29-35: Jacob "earns" two wives.

Tamar: Genesis 38.

Rahab: Joshua 2:1-21; Hebrews 11:31; James 2:25.

Ruth: The Book of Ruth.

Bathsheba: 2 Samuel 11.

FIRST WEEK OF ADVENT

PRAYER SERVICE FOR THE FIRST WEEK OF ADVENT

<u>THEME:</u> Watchfulness

<u>GATHERING RITUAL:</u> Come together in a dimly lighted room, seated around a bare (uncovered) table on which has been placed a large bare branch and one unlit candle.

<u>FOCUS TIME:</u> A moment of silence accompanied by background music; could be followed by an advent song such as "O Come, O Come, Emmanuel."

Leader: There shall come forth a shoot from the stump of Jesse. And a branch shall grow out of these roots (cf. Isaiah 11:1).

Reader 1: Come, let us go to the mountain of God, to the house of the God of our ancestors, the God of Abraham and Sarah, the God of Isaac and Rebekah, the God of Jacob and Rachel and Leah, that God may instruct us in divine ways and that we may walk in God's paths (cf. Isaiah 2:3).

All: MAKE US TURN TO YOU, O GOD. LET US SEE YOUR FACE AND WE SHALL BE SAVED (cf. Missal, Cycle B).

Reader 2: O, that you, God, would rend the heavens and come down, that you might meet us doing right, that we were mindful of you in our ways (cf. Isaiah 63:19; 64:4).

All: MAKE US TURN TO YOU, O GOD. LET US SEE YOUR FACE AND WE SHALL BE SAVED.

Reader 3: Once again, O God, look upon us and see. Take care of this vine and protect what your right hand has planted (cf. Psalm 80).

All: MAKE US TURN TO YOU, O GOD. LET US SEE YOUR FACE AND WE SHALL BE SAVED.

Leader: There shall come forth a shoot from the stump of Jesse. And a branch shall grow out of these roots (cf. Isaiah 11:1).

7

GOSPEL READING: [A single candle is lighted; read Matthew 24:37-44 (cf. Cycle A).]

The coming of God will repeat what happened in Noah's time. In the days before the flood people were eating and drinking, marrying and being married, right up to the day Noah entered the ark. They were totally unconcerned until the flood came and destroyed them. So it will be at the coming of God. Two men will be out in the field; one will be taken and one will be left. Two women are grinding at the mill; one will be taken and one will be left. Stay awake, therefore! You cannot know the day your God is coming.

Be sure of this: if the owners of the house knew when the thief was coming they would keep a watchful eye and not allow their house to be broken into. You must be prepared in the same way. Your God is coming at the time you least expect.

[Pause here for a few moments of silence.]
[The following could be delivered aloud or read silently.]

WAKE UP! BE WATCHFUL! COME, CLIMB THE MOUNTAIN OF GOD! COME INTO THE LIGHT OF GOD'S HOUSE, TO THE PLACE WHERE GOD DWELLS. Why? So that God may instruct us—that we might dwell in God's ways. Mountain-climbing takes time, effort, and courage; it takes a certain amount of watchfulness, of mindfulness, lest we slide backward, downhill. In the season of Advent, we are called to mindfulness, to watchfulness in the midst of frenzied activity, to quiet ourselves in the midst of our darkness, to be vigilant, to make ready for the coming of light. As days grow shorter and colder and winter's nights keep us indoors for security and warmth, the Church invites us to turn our minds and hearts inward, to reflect on our lives and the journey we have begun.

In this winter season when the sap settles into the roots of the trees, Advent requires that we settle into our own roots, that we listen to the deepest longings of our hearts

(Stuhmueller, *Meditations for Advent and the Christmas Season*, p.ix). It calls us to that place where God dwells within us so that we might be alert to the mysterious presence of God in our world. In Noah's time, the opportunity for salvation came when people were busy with their own plans. They were so immersed in the flow of ordinary events that they were blind to the moment of opportunity. Caught up in their own pursuits, they were surprised by the flood, and they perished. In Matthew's Gospel, Jesus uses two pairs of workers to describe what it will be like at the coming of God. Two men are working in a field; two women are grinding meal. The situations look alike, yet one man and one woman will be taken, and one of each will be left. The coming of God brings to light distinctions between persons; it promises reward for those who are vigilant even in the midst of routine or hectic activity. If we are not vigilant, if we rush too quickly toward Christmas, if we are totally unconcerned, mindlessly eating and drinking and sleeping—working in the fields or grinding meal—shopping and decorating and baking and cleaning, buying presents and meeting deadlines, if we continue our routine without mindfulness, without expectation and hope, we risk repeating what happened on that first Christmas.

The mystery will pass us by. The coming of God will take place outside our consciousness, just as the birth of Jesus took place outside the inns of Bethlehem because there was no room in the minds and hearts of a people taken by surprise. God often comes in surprise packages. If we are not watchful, we will not detect the hints and signals. We will not notice that God is trying desperately to break into our lives, knocking at the door, trying to be born in our hearts. Will we make room?

Advent challenges us to prepare for the unexpected, for the sprouting of roots hidden deep within us and within our history, to be ready for the coming of God that will take us most by surprise, to pay attention, to wait in patience for one who is already in our midst.

[Pause for silent response.]

DISCUSSION/REFLECTION:

Who are the people who have served as hidden roots that have inspired us, nurtured us in our youth or early childhood?

When in our lives has God brought forth a tender shoot, a living branch, where we least expected it?

What hidden treasures will we pass on to the next generation?

CLOSING PRAYER:

Leader: There shall come forth a shoot from the stump of Jesse. And a branch shall grow out of these roots (cf. Isaiah 11:1).

Reader 1: Come, let us go to the mountain of God, to the house of the God of our ancestors, the God of Abraham and Sarah, the God of Isaac and Rebekah, the God of Jacob, and Rachel and Leah, that God may instruct us in divine ways and that we may walk in God's paths (cf. Isaiah 2:3).

All: MAKE US TURN TO YOU, O GOD. LET US SEE YOUR FACE AND WE SHALL BE SAVED (cf. Missal, Cycle B).

Leader: With our ancestors, Abraham and Sarah who welcomed the surprise visit from God in human form to their tent at Mamre and who laughed at the unexpected gift of God (Genesis 17,18), let us welcome the surprise visits of God in the persons of the needy who come unexpectedly into our lives this Advent.

All: MAKE US TURN TO YOU, O GOD. LET US SEE YOUR FACE AND WE SHALL BE SAVED.

Leader: Let us recall in grateful praise our foremothers and forefathers, those hidden roots who have nourished us and inspired us. [Here allow time for all to mention names.]

Leader: Make us turn to you, O God.

All: MAKE US TURN TO YOU, O GOD. LET US SEE YOUR FACE AND WE SHALL BE SAVED.

Leader: Let us carry with us this week a reminder of these hidden roots; let us hope for sprouting branches where we least expect them, and let us nourish the tender shoots among us.

All: MAKE US TURN TO YOU, O GOD. LET US SEE YOUR FACE AND WE
        SHALL BE SAVED.

Leader: There shall come forth a shoot from the stump of
        Jesse. And a branch shall grow out of these roots.

CLOSING SONG: "O Come, O Come, Emmanuel."
[During the song, each participant takes a small twig from the
branch to keep as a reminder of our hidden roots and as a
symbol of hope in God's promise that new life will spring up
where we least expect it.]

SECOND WEEK OF ADVENT

The readings selected for the Sundays and weekdays of Advent rely heavily upon the writings of the Hebrew prophets, particularly the prophet Isaiah. In all three Cycles (A,B,C) the Gospel readings for the Second and Third Sundays of Advent focus on the prophetic ministry of John the Baptist. Prophets are those who speak the word of God to their contemporaries; they are "seers," those who see more clearly than others the implications of certain events and who articulate for their own generation the meaning of those events. From our vantage point and from that of the authors of the New Testament, Christians look back to the Hebrew Scriptures and read into their stories and events the Advent themes of promise and fulfillment.

Themes from the readings for the first week of Advent continue into the second week: AWAKE! BE WATCHFUL! GET READY! SURPRISE! A SHOOT SHALL SPROUT! In all three cycles, the Synoptic Gospel readings for Sunday of Week Two feature John the Baptist quoting the prophet Isaiah,

"A voice of one crying out in the
desert:
'Prepare the way of the Lord,
make straight his paths. . . .'" (Luke 3:4**).
In Cycle B we read: But the day of the Lord will come like a thief, . . . (2 Peter 3:10**). In the first reading for Cycle A, Isaiah's message from Week One is repeated,
"A shoot shall sprout from the stump of Jesse,
and from his roots a bud shall blossom."

PRAYER SERVICE FOR THE SECOND WEEK OF ADVENT

THEME: Roots—Prophetic and Natural

GATHERING RITUAL: Come together, as for Week One, in a dimly lighted room, seated around a bare (uncovered) table on which has been placed a large bare branch along with pine cones, dried leaves and two unlit candles.

FOCUS TIME: A moment of silence accompanied by background music; could be followed by an Advent song such as "On Jordan's Bank."

Leader: A shoot shall sprout from the stump of Jesse, and from these roots a bud shall blossom (cf. Isaiah 11:1).

Reader 1: A voice cries out: In the desert prepare the way of the Lord. Make straight in the wasteland a highway for our God! Every valley shall be filled in, every mountain and hill shall be made low. The rugged land shall be made a plain, the rough country a broad valley. Then the glory of God shall be revealed and all humankind shall see it together (cf. Isaiah 40:3-5, Cycle B).

All: O GOD, LET US SEE YOUR KINDNESS AND RECOGNIZE YOUR SALVATION.

Reader 2: Then the wolf shall be the guest of the lamb, and the leopard shall lie down with the kid; the calf and the young lion shall browse together, with a little child to guide them. . . . The baby shall play by the cobra's den, and the child lay her hand on the adder's lair (cf. Isaiah 11:6-8, Cycle A).

All: O GOD, LET US SEE YOUR KINDNESS AND RECOGNIZE YOUR SALVATION.

Reader 3: There shall be no harm or ruin on all my holy mountain; for the earth shall be filled with the knowledge of God, as water covers the sea. On that day, the root of Jesse, set up as a signal for the nations, the Gentiles shall seek out, for God's coming shall be glorious (cf. Isaiah 11:9,10, Cycle A).

All: O GOD, LET US SEE YOUR KINDNESS AND RECOGNIZE YOUR SALVATION.

GOSPEL READING: [Two candles are lighted.]

A reading from the Gospel of Luke. [Read Luke 3:2-6 (cf. Cycle C).]

And the word of God came to John, son of Zechariah [and Elizabeth] in the desert. He went about the whole region of the Jordan, proclaiming a baptism of repentance for the forgiveness of sins, as it is written in the words of the prophet Isaiah, "A voice of one crying out in the desert:

Prepare the way of the Lord,
Clear a straight path.
Every valley shall be filled
And every mountain and hill made low.
Winding roads shall be made straight
And the rough ways smooth.
And all flesh shall see the salvation of God."

[Pause here for a few moments of silence.]
[The following could be delivered aloud or read silently.]

"Prepare! Make straight paths; fill the valleys. . . .
Level the mountains!"

Images of nature appear throughout the readings for this week: a desert wasteland, broad valleys and lofty mountains, rugged lands, gorges and level grounds, night and day, east and west, the River Jordan, wolf and lamb, leopard and kid, forests and trees. "A shoot shall sprout . . . a bud shall blossom."

Ancient peoples had a healthy respect for nature. Even as they feared the dark and the cold and the winds, they were acutely aware of the relationship between nature and human well-being. They appreciated the sun and the rain and the earth. Trees were often revered as symbolic of motherhood, of rebirth and new life (Walker, p. 39). The plant and animal worlds were celebrated in recognition of their essential contribution to the survival of human life. So also the prophet Isaiah uses symbols from the natural environment to describe the advent of God among the peoples of the earth. After centuries of darkness and waiting, the land must be made ready, the desert prepared, for a shoot shall sprout from a stump and a bud shall blossom. And in those days the whole earth will be restored; people everywhere will live in harmony, and all humankind shall see the salvation of God.

Advent calls us to participate in this rebirth, to return to our roots, to show a healthy respect for all of God's creation, to live more peacefully where we are planted, to be more at home with ourselves and to prepare our hearts as well as our land for rebirth and reconciliation, to make God present in our world and in our relationships. It calls us to be prophetic in our own time, to declare to one another the coming of God in our midst. It calls us to reflect, to watch, to sink into our own depths and to allow the message growing within us to burst forth even in the midst of confusion, of dissonant voices and frenzied activity, of gloomy days and long nights, of mountains and valleys, of rough and rugged wastelands. We must become the advent of God in our contemporary world.

Let us cry out from the rugged land and from the mountain top, "Here is our God!" Let us reach back to the very beginning of our religious history and, with the "prophet Miriam and all the women who went out after her, with timbrels and dancing" (cf. Exodus 15:20), from our own desert wilderness, "Sing to God who is gloriously triumphant . . . who has become our salvation" (cf. Exodus 15:21,22). Let us season our lives and our culture with an awareness of God's coming. O God, let us see your kindness and recognize your salvation.

[Pause for silent response.]

DISCUSSION/REFLECTION:

The readings for this week use symbols from the natural environment of the holy land to express the meaning of God's coming. What symbols from nature make us aware of God's presence in our world?

How is God's presence manifest in the events of our country, our neighborhood, our families, and our individual lives?

What promise for our future does this Advent hold?

CLOSING PRAYER

Leader: A shoot shall sprout from the stump of Jesse, and from these roots a bud shall blossom.

All: ALL HUMANKIND SHALL SEE THE GLORY OF GOD.

Reader 1: Everything written before our time was written for our instruction, that we might derive hope from the lessons of patience and the words of encouragement in the scriptures. May God, the source of all patience and encouragement, enable us to live in perfect harmony with one another according to the spirit of Christ Jesus, so that with one heart and voice we may glorify God (cf. Romans 15:4,5).

All: ALL HUMANKIND SHALL SEE THE GLORY OF GOD.

Reader 2: And this is my prayer: that your love may increase ever more and more in knowledge and every kind of perception, to discern what is of value, so that you may be pure and blameless for the day of Christ, ... for the glory and praise of God (Philippians 1:9-11**).

All: ALL HUMANKIND SHALL SEE THE GLORY OF GOD.

CLOSING SONG: "O Come, Thou Root of Jesse, Come" (verse from "O Come, O Come, Emmanuel").

[During the song, each participant takes a pine cone to be used at home with the Advent/Christmas decorations as a reminder to look for God in nature and in the ordinary events of life.]

ADDITIONAL SUGGESTED READINGS: Women named as prophets in the Hebrew Scriptures:

Miriam: Exodus 15; Numbers 12
Deborah: Judges 4,5
Hulda II: Kings 22:14-20; II Chronicles 34
Noadiah: Nehemiah 6:14

THIRD WEEK OF ADVENT

Traditionally known as Gaudete Sunday, the third Sunday of Advent derives this Latin name from the opening word of the Entrance Antiphon, "REJOICE!" The readings suggest cause for rejoicing, for joyful hope. All three Gospels (Cycles A,B,C) focus on John the Baptist and his prophecy concerning the One Who Is To Come, Who Is Among Us, Whom We Do Not Recognize. In Luke (Cycle C), the crowds ask John, "What ought we to do?" And John responds, "Let those with two coats give to those who have none. Anyone who has food should do the same." And in Matthew (Cycle A), the signs of God's coming are made clear by the words of Jesus,

> Blind people recover their sight; those who are crip-
> pled walk; people with leprosy are cured; those who
> are deaf hear; dead people are raised to life; and those
> who are poor have the good news preached to them
> (Matthew 11:5).

Jesus adds a word of caution, "And blessed are those who find no stumbling block in me" (cf. Matthew 11:6).

Sunday's first reading in each cycle is chosen to reinforce the theme of the Gospel,

> Then will the eyes of the blind be
>   opened, . . . (Isaiah 35:5**, Cycle A);
>   . . . glad tidings to the lowly, . . ."(Isaiah 61:1**, Cycle B);
>   . . . no further misfortune to fear (Zephaniah 3:15**, Cycle

C). And in Cycles B and C the Pauline readings open with the word, "Rejoice."

PRAYER SERVICE FOR THE THIRD WEEK OF ADVENT

THEME: Good Tidings to the Lowly

GATHERING RITUAL: Come together as in previous weeks in a dimly lighted room, seated around a bare (uncovered) table on which lies a large bare branch surrounded by sprigs of holly and three unlit candles.

FOCUS TIME: [A moment of silence accompanied by background music such as Beethoven's "Ode to Joy."]

17

Leader: "A shoot shall sprout from the stump of Jesse, and from these roots a bud shall blossom."

Reader 1: The spirit of God is upon me, because God has anointed me; God has sent me to bring glad tidings to the lowly, to heal the brokenhearted, to proclaim liberty to the captives and release to the prisoners, to announce a year of favor from God (cf. Isaiah 61:1-2, Cycle B).

All: REJOICE ALWAYS! AGAIN I SAY REJOICE!

Reader 2: I rejoice heartily . . . God is the joy of my soul; for God has clothed me with a robe of salvation. As the earth brings forth its plants, and a garden makes its growth spring up, so will God make justice and praise spring up before all the nations (cf. Isaiah 61:10,11).

All: REJOICE ALWAYS! AGAIN I SAY REJOICE!

GOSPEL READING: [Three candles are lighted; read Matthew 11:2-11, cf. Cycle A.]

When John heard in prison about the works of the Messiah, he sent his disciples to him with this question, "Are you the one who is to come or shall we look for another?" Jesus said to them in reply, "Go and tell John what you see and hear: blind people recover their sight, those who are lame walk, people with leprosy are cleansed, those who are deaf hear, the dead are raised to life, and the poor have the good news preached to them. Blessed are they who find no stumbling block in me."

As the messengers set off, Jesus began to speak to the crowds about John. "What did you go out to the desert to see? A reed swayed by the wind? Tell me, what did you go out to see? Someone dressed in fine clothing? Those who wear fine clothing are in royal palaces. Why then did you go out? To see a prophet? Yes, I tell you, a prophet indeed and more than a prophet. This is the one about whom it is written, 'I am sending my messenger ahead of you; he will prepare your way before you.'"

I solemnly assure you, among those born of women there has been none greater than John the Baptist; yet the least in the reign of God is greater.

[Pause here for a few moments of silence.]
[The following could be delivered aloud or read silently.]

Advent brings good tidings to those who long for the fulfillment of God's promise. Salvation comes to those who wait in joyful expectation as an expectant mother rejoices while preparing for the child who is already in her womb. In Advent we watch and prepare for One Who is Already In Our Midst. Hear the words of Zephaniah from the first reading for Sunday, Cycle C:

Shout for joy, O daughter Zion. . . . Your God is in your
midst. . . . Fear not, O Zion, be not discouraged . . .
God will rejoice over you with gladness (cf.
Zephaniah 3:14-18).

They are echoed in the angel's greeting to Mary in the Annunciation scene as recorded in Luke's Gospel:

Rejoice, O favored one, the Lord is with you. Do not be
afraid, for you have found favor with God (cf. Luke 1:28-30).

The angel's announcement to Mary took her by surprise. Yet, because of her hope in God's promise and the nourishment of her Jewish tradition, Mary was able to say, "YES! I am ready." She knew well the stories of her foremothers who gave birth in unusual, even miraculous circumstances. She remembered Sarah who laughed when she learned that she would bear a child in her old age, and Rebekah who remained childless for some time until God, in answer to prayer, blessed her with twins. She would have remembered also the story of Rachel who, distraught over her long wait for a child, cried out, "Give me children or else I die" (cf. Genesis 30:1). And Luke indicates that Mary was familiar with the story of Hannah, a woman of prayer and mother of Samuel, who had been deeply distressed by the "infertility" of her youth.

On one of Hannah's annual pilgrimages with her husband to the shrine at Shiloh, she vowed that, if she were blessed with a son, she would give him back to God "all the days of his life" (cf. I Samuel 1:11). And after God had granted her request, when the child had been weaned, Hannah took him to the temple. There, fulfilling her vow, she dedicated her son to

God. Her prayer of thanksgiving and praise to God, handed on as the "Song of Hannah," inspired Mary's Song of Praise, the Magnificat (Luke 1:46-55).

Used as the responsorial psalm for this Sunday in Cycle B, Mary's Song of Praise seems to summarize our themes for this week's reflection. It rejoices in God's favor for those who make ready for God's coming, who find room in their hearts for the fulfillment of God's promise. It is good tidings for the lowly, suggesting the signs by which Elizabeth's son, John, would later recognize the coming of God (Matthew 11:2-6).

[Pause for silent response.]

DISCUSSION/REFLECTION: The readings for this Sunday invite us to make room in our hearts for God's presence in our lives.

What demands does this invitation make on our daily routine?

What stumbling blocks does our culture place on this Advent path?

What activities/events in our culture can we incorporate into our observance of Advent?

CLOSING PRAYER:
Leader: A shoot shall sprout from the stump of Jesse, and from these roots a bud shall blossom.
Reader 1: My soul proclaims the greatness of God, my spirit finds joy in God, my savior, for you have looked upon your servant in my lowliness; all ages to come shall call me blessed.
All: MY SPIRIT REJOICES IN GOD MY SAVIOR.
Reader 2: God, you are mighty, and you have done great things for me, holy is your name; your mercy is from age to age on those who fear you.
All: MY SPIRIT REJOICES IN GOD MY SAVIOR.
Reader 3: The hungry you have given every good thing, while the rich are sent empty away. You have upheld Israel your servant, ever mindful of your mercy.
All: MY SPIRIT REJOICES IN GOD MY SAVIOR.

CLOSING SONG: "Ode to Joy" or "Rejoice Always in the Lord." [Each participant takes a sprig of holly, ancient symbol of life surviving the barrenness of winter, its red berries a reminder of the hidden root from which a bud shall blossom.]

FOURTH WEEK OF ADVENT

Memories of Jesus included in the Gospels began with an oral tradition which originated in the proclamation of the Resurrection. This was followed by stories of the Passion and Death. As the oral tradition continued, memories of the public ministry were added. These form the major portion of all four canonical Gospels, and it is generally believed that the stories included there, although shaped by the memories of the early community and adapted by each evangelist for a particular purpose, are based on remembered historical events.

In contrast, the infancy narratives, found at the beginning of the Gospels of Matthew and Luke, have been recognized by scholars as a form of Jewish literature known as *midrash*, an artful combination of scriptural themes and contemporary interpretation (Senior, *Invitation to Matthew*, p. 33). They were added to the Gospels of Matthew and Luke at a later date. The Gospels of Mark and John do not include stories of the birth and infancy.

All the Gospel readings for the fourth week, daily and Sunday, are taken from these infancy narratives of Matthew and Luke. They take shape from the writings of the prophets which the Christian community has interpreted as being fulfilled in the coming of Jesus as Messiah. They have been called miniature Gospels because they carry within themselves the main message of each evangelist.

The Sunday Gospel for Cycle A is taken from Matthew. It approaches the annunciation of the conception of Jesus from the perspective of Joseph. Members of Matthew's community, aware of their roots in Judaism, seek to establish their identity as Christian missionaries. A major purpose of Matthew's Gospel is to establish the continuity of the Gospel of Jesus with the Jewish tradition and with the fulfillment of Jewish prophecy. In this first chapter, he establishes a theme repeated throughout his Gospel, "All this happened to fulfill what God had spoken through the prophet" (cf. Matthew 1:22).

The Sunday Gospels for Cycles B and C are taken from Luke. They present the more familiar stories of the annunciation to Mary and of her visit to her cousin Elizabeth. The Christian community to whom Luke's Gospel is addressed was made up of gentiles who were further removed from the origins of Christianity. Luke wrote to reassure his readers concerning the foundations of Christian living. While Matthew is concerned with the legal origins of Jesus as a Jew, Luke is concerned with the message of Jesus as model for Christian living. He approaches the conception and birth from the perspective of Mary, model disciple for all Christians.

PRAYER SERVICE FOR THE FOURTH WEEK OF ADVENT

THEME: Birthing

GATHERING RITUAL: Come together as in other weeks in a dimly lighted room, seated around a bare (uncovered) table on which have been placed a large bare branch, some holly leaves, four unlit candles, and a vase of fresh buds.

FOCUS TIME: A moment of silence accompanied by background music, such as the traditional carol, "Lo, How a Rose."

Leader: "A shoot shall sprout from the stump of Jesse, and from these roots a bud shall blossom."

Reader 1: Rejoice, O highly favored daughter! Our God is with you. Blessed are you among women (cf. Luke1:28,42).

All: REJOICE, MARY! YOU ARE BLESSED AMONG WOMEN.

Reader 2: Do not fear, Mary, you have found favor with God. You shall conceive and bear a child whose name will be called Jesus. Great will be his dignity, and he will be called Child of the Most High (cf. Luke1:30,31).

All: REJOICE, MARY! YOU ARE BLESSED AMONG WOMEN.

Reader 3: The Holy Spirit will come upon you and the power of God will overshadow you; hence, your holy offspring will be called the Son of God (cf. Luke 1:35).

ALL: REJOICE, MARY! YOU ARE BLESSED AMONG WOMEN.

Reader 4: I am the handmaid of God. Let it be done as you say (cf. Luke1:38).

All: REJOICE, MARY! YOU ARE BLESSED AMONG WOMEN.

GOSPEL READING: [All four candles are lighted; read Luke 1:39-45, cf. Cycle C]

> Mary set out, proceeding in haste into the hill country to a town of Judah, where she entered the house of Zechariah and Elizabeth. When Elizabeth heard Mary's greeting, the baby stirred in her womb. Elizabeth was filled with the Holy Spirit and cried out in a loud voice, "Blessed are you among women and blessed is the fruit of your womb. And who am I that the mother of my Lord should come to me? For at the moment the sound of your greeting reached my ears, the infant in my womb leaped for joy. Blessed are you who trusted that God's word to you would be fulfilled."

[Pause here for a few moments of silence.]
[The following could be delivered aloud or read silently.]

"Blessed is she who trusted that God's word to her would be fulfilled."

The encounter of these two pregnant women embodies the mission of every Christian, to give birth to the Word of God that dwells within us. Such birthing is possible only through the power of the God's Spirit. As Mary, pregnant with the Word of God, greets her expectant cousin, the babe in Elizabeth's womb leaps for joy in the power of the Holy Spirit. And Elizabeth cries out, "Who am I that the mother of my Lord should come to me?" We witness in both these women the fruits of the Holy Spirit. We find a spirit of courage and joy, of openness and gratitude, of deep faith and generosity, and of utter, yet humble conviction that God's word will be fulfilled in them.

The lectionary reading begins by stating that Mary set out, "proceeding in haste" into the hill country, to a town of Judah. The Jerusalem Bible reads, "Mary went as quickly as she could." Now, anyone who has traveled that general route from Nazareth to the hill country outside Jerusalem knows that, even today, you go only "as quickly as you can" and, if you are on a donkey or traveling by foot, it takes several days to journey from the hills of Galilee, across the plains, through the mountains of Samaria, and finally into the Judean hillside. The journey implies that Mary's spontaneous response to the surprise plan of God for her impelled her also to reach out to Elizabeth in human solidarity in the face of a mystery of faith that neither understood, but in which they both trusted.

We are beneficiaries of Luke's account of that encounter; it is part of a living tradition that informs and stirs our imagination, capable of leading us toward creative and positive responses to the surprise visits and promptings of God's Spirit in our own lives. Our sacred words are spoken in the holy places of our daily lives. We hold a tradition and a promise in our hearts just as Mary carried her treasure from Nazareth to the home of Elizabeth and Zechariah in the hill country of Judah. At appropriate moments we too are called to burst forth in praise of God, in words of comfort and promise to the poor and oppressed, in words of challenge to the proud and of confrontation to the powerful, words of joy and love, of empowerment and blessing to each other.

[Pause for silent response.]

DISCUSSION/REFLECTION: Mary and Elizabeth may be thought of as the first Christians.

What qualities distinguish them as model disciples?

Where are the holy places in our town or community?

Who are the blessed ones who inform and nurture the life of God's spirit in us?

To what word of God are we called to give birth this advent?

CLOSING PRAYER:

Leader: "A shoot shall sprout from the stump of Jesse, and from these roots a bud shall blossom."

Reader: To God who is able to strengthen you in the gospel which I proclaim when I preach Christ Jesus, the gospel which reveals the mystery hidden for many ages but now manifested through the writings of the prophets, and, at the command of the eternal God, made known to all the gentiles that they may believe and obey, to God who alone is wise, may glory be given through Jesus Christ unto endless ages (cv. Romans 16:25-27, Cycle B)."

All: A SHOOT SHALL SPROUT FROM THE STUMP OF JESSE, AND FROM THESE ROOTS A BUD SHALL BLOSSOM.

CLOSING SONG: "O Come, O Come, Emmanuel" or "Lo How a Rose."

[Each participant takes a bud from the vase as a reminder that we are all expected to give birth to the hidden word of God that is planted within our hearts.]

FEASTS OF THE CHRISTMAS SEASON

As noted earlier, the celebration of Christmas is rooted in nature's annual cycle of darkness and light. With the coming of the winter solstice in the Northern Hemisphere, the long dark nights gradually give way to increasing rays of sunlight and length of days. So each year when the day of the solstice finally arrives, at the moment when "the sun stands still," Christians proclaim that Christ, the Son Of God and Light Of The World, breaks into our earth, into our humanity. A season of great joy and festivity replaces the period of watchfulness and anticipation.

Toward the end of the third century, the Roman Emperor declared December 25, the calendar date of the winter solstice, to be celebrated as the Feast of the Invincible Sun, marking the triumph of day over night. By the middle of the next century, the Christians in Rome were keeping that same day as the festival of the birth of Christ, the "Sun of righteousness" (Simcoe, ed., *Parish Path through Advent and Christmastime*, p.3). In the Eastern churches, at least by the end of the fourth century, January 6 was kept as the feast of Christ's birth or Epiphany. It celebrated, along with the birth of Jesus in human form, the revelation of his divinity at his baptism by John and in the miracle at Cana. Both feast days, December 25 and January 6, gradually came to be kept throughout the entire Christian world, with the intervening days known as the "twelve days of Christmas."

In this Christmas season, we stand in awe before the birth of a child. Surrounded by darkness, we have seen "a great light, a child has been born for us whose name is Wonder-Counselor, God-Hero, Prince of Peace" (cf. Isaiah 9: 1-6). Along with Mary, we ponder these things in our hearts. Along with her we do not isolate the human birth from the manifestation of divinity, the babe in Bethlehem from the adult Christ in Galilee and Jerusalem, the birth from the cross and resurrection. This child, born of Mary, is also divine. This child is the Savior of the world and so we see in this birth the shadow of the cross, as well as the light of Resurrection. Christmas is the feast of Incarnation, of God become Human for the purpose of making us human beings more like God.

THE FEAST OF CHRISTMAS

(THE FEAST OF THE SOLEMNITY OF MARY, MOTHER OF GOD)

PRAYER SERVICE FOR THE FEAST OF CHRISTMAS

THEME: Christ, Our Light, The Savior Of The World is born.

GATHERING RITUAL: Come together in a room decorated for Christmas, perhaps around a manger scene or a fireplace or a Christmas tree, with one large lighted candle. Burning incense and flowers would also be appropriate.

FOCUS TIME: A moment of silence followed by singing of a Christmas carol, such as "Angels We Have Heard On High."

Leader: A light has shone on us this day.
All: A LIGHT HAS SHONE ON US THIS DAY.
Leader: The people who walked in darkness
      have seen a great light;
        Upon those who dwelt in the land
        of gloom
        a light has shone (Isaiah 9:1**).
All: A LIGHT HAS SHONE ON US THIS DAY.
Leader: You have brought them abundant
         joy
        and great rejoicing, . . .
      For the yoke that burdened them,
        the pole on their shoulder,
      And the rod of their taskmaster
        you have smashed, as on the day
        of Midian (Isaiah 9:2,3**).
All: A LIGHT HAS SHONE ON US THIS DAY.
Leader: For a child is born to us, a son is
        given us;
        upon his shoulder dominion rests.
      They name him Wonder-Counselor,
        God-Hero,
        . . . Prince of Peace.
      His dominion is vast
        and forever peaceful, . . . (Isaiah 9:5,6**).
All: A LIGHT HAS SHONE ON US THIS DAY.

GOSPEL READING: [cf. Luke 2:1-20 (selected verses)]

    In those days, . . . while they were [in Bethlehem], the days of Mary's confinement were completed. She gave birth to her firstborn son and wrapped him in swaddling clothes and laid him in a manger, because there was no room for them in the place where travelers lodged.

    Now there were shepherds in the locality, keeping night watch by turns over their flock when an angel appeared to them and the glory of God shone round about them, and they were very much afraid. The angel said to them, "Do not be afraid. I come to proclaim good news to you, tidings of great joy to be shared by all the people. This day is born to you a savior. In David's city, in a manger, you will find an infant wrapped in swaddling clothes". . . . So the shepherds went in haste and found Mary and Joseph and the baby.

    Once they saw, they understood what had been told them concerning the child. The shepherds glorified God for all they had heard and seen and all who heard of it wondered at what the shepherds told them. But Mary kept all these things, pondering them in her heart.

[Pause for a few moments of silence, followed by singing a Christmas carol, such as "Glory to God in the Highest."]
[The following could be delivered aloud or read silently.]

"Mary treasured all these things and reflected
on them in her heart."

    In this scene presented by Luke, an angel appears from heaven proclaiming tidings of great joy; the shepherds go "in haste" to Bethlehem, the ancestral city of David's family, where they "saw and understood what had been told them concerning the child." Having seen and understood, the shepherds glorify God and proclaim to others what they have seen and heard. This pericope, reminiscent of related events in the life of Mary, suggests that the content of Mary's reflection includes not only the awe and mystery of the present moment, but the meaning of past events and prayerful wonder concerning the future.

The Angel Gabriel had said to Mary, "Do not be afraid, . . . you have found favor with God . . . the child to be born to you will be called holy, the son of God" (cf. Luke 1:30,35). And Mary, like the shepherds, had gone "with haste" into the hill country to a city of Judah where she shared her good news with her cousin Elizabeth, who also saw and understood, "Blessed are you among women, and blessed is the fruit of your womb." And Mary's response to Elizabeth had given glory to God in the beautiful words of the Magnificat, "My soul gives glory to God, for the one who is mighty has done great things for me and holy is God's name."

As Mary's thoughts turn again to reflection and praise of God for the mighty works done in her presence and in her life, Luke's community would be mindful also of another event in the life of Mary and her Son.

"As he said this, a woman in the crowd raised her voice"and said to [Jesus], "Blessed is the womb that bore you and the breasts that nursed you." But Jesus replied,

> "Blessed rather are those who hear the word of God and keep it" (cf. Luke 11: 27).

Mary is blessed by God and praised by her son, not because she gave him birth and nursed him, but because she "hears the word of God and keeps it."

We, like Mary, treasure this mystery of Christmas that takes shape in our hearts. We are struck by the irony of divine splendor and human poverty. We are struck by the heavenly proclamation of angels contrasted with the stark simplicity of poor shepherds who see and believe; by the royal city of Bethlehem proclaimed as the birthplace of the Messiah, compared to the humble lodging which had no room for Mary to give him birth. We are surprised by this divine child, born of woman; by this Word Made Flesh; by this God become human so that we might become like God. We, like Mary, allow the child within us to pause in awe and wonder at the marvelous things that have come to pass. We, like Mary, ponder these things in our hearts, and we too are blessed when we hear the word of God—ponder it, treasure it, and keep it—not just at Christmastime, but at every moment of our lives.

[Pause for silent response.]

DISCUSSION/REFLECTION: What have we seen and heard?

CLOSING SONG: "Angels We Have Heard on High," "Go Tell it on the Mountain," or another favorite Christmas carol.

[Participants could exchange small, inexpensive gifts or symbols related to the theme, followed by light refreshments.]

THE FEAST WITHIN THE OCTAVE

For the most part, the readings are the same for all three liturgical cycles. They remind us that Christmas is not just a commemoration of past events, but the celebration of God With Us now and always. The Gospels focus on events surrounding the birth and growth to adulthood of the human Jesus. The infancy narratives of Matthew and Luke are theological presentations rather than historical records. They are intended to inspire the early Christian communities to grow in faith as they hear again and again the word of God and learn, along with Mary, how to treasure it and live it out.

In the selections that follow, we reflect on the Gospels through the eyes of Mary. For the week immediately following Christmas we choose selections from the Gospel of Luke for Cycles B and C. This Sunday, traditionally celebrated as the Feast of the Holy Family, uses the same scripture passages for the first and second readings each year. The Gospel for Cycle A is the account by Matthew of the flight of Mary and Joseph with the baby Jesus into Egypt. Luke's stories of the presentation of Jesus in the temple and the finding of Jesus in the temple are used respectively in Cycles B and C.

On January 1, the Octave of Christmas, the Church celebrates the Solemnity of Mary, Mother of God. The Gospel for all three cycles is that of Luke which was used also for the Mass at Dawn on Christmas Day. In this guide, the reflection and prayer service suggested for the Feast of Christmas includes this passage from Luke. Since this week provides an abundance of feasts and celebrations from which to choose for a weekly gathering, it is assumed that the one service will suffice as a guide for this feast as well.

On January 6 or on the Sunday between January 2 and 8, the Church celebrates the solemnity of the Epiphany. The liturgical readings are the same for all three cycles. The Gospel of Matthew presents the visit of astrologers from the East, the Magi. It tells how the birth of the Jewish Messiah was revealed to them, signaling salvation for gentiles as well.

The reflections here will look through the eyes of Mary at the meaning of these events.

PRAYER SERVICE FOR THE FEAST WITHIN THE OCTAVE OF CHRISTMAS

THEME: Journeys to Jerusalem's Temple

GATHERING RITUAL: Gather, as on the Feast of Christmas, in a room decorated for the season with one large lighted candle representing Christ, the light of the world.

FOCUS TIME: A moment of silence followed by singing of a Christmas carol.

Leader: [A reading from the Gospel of Luke 2:22-52 (cf. select-ed passages).]
> And when the time came . . . Mary and Joseph brought Jesus up to Jerusalem to present him to the Lord. . . to do for him according to the custom of the law. . . .
> Now there was a man in Jerusalem whose name was Simeon, righteous and devout, and looking for the consolation of Israel. . . . And inspired by the Spirit, he came into the temple; and when Mary and Joseph brought in the child Jesus, . . . he took him up into his arms and blessed God, and said,

All: *NOW YOU CAN LET YOUR SERVANT GO IN PEACE JUST AS YOU PROMISED; BECAUSE MY EYES HAVE SEEN THE SALVATION WHICH YOU HAVE PREPARED FOR ALL THE NATIONS TO SEE. A LIGHT TO ENLIGHTEN THE GENTILES AND THE GLORY OF YOUR PEOPLE ISRAEL.*

Leader: And his father and his mother marveled at what was said about him; and Simeon blessed them and said to Mary, his mother,

All: *BEHOLD, THIS CHILD IS SET FOR THE FALL AND RISE OF MANY IN ISRAEL, AND FOR A SIGN THAT WILL BE REJECTED. AND A SWORD WILL PIERCE YOUR OWN SOUL TOO, THAT THE SECRET THOUGHTS OF MANY MAY BE REVEALED.*

Leader: And there was a prophetess, Anna; she was of a great age. . . . She did not depart from the temple, worshiping with fasting and prayer night and day. And coming up at that very hour, she gave thanks to God, and spoke of this Child to all who were looking for the redemption of Israel.

And when they had performed everything according to the law, they returned to Galilee, to their own city, Nazareth. And the child grew and became strong, filled with wisdom; and the favor of God was upon him.

[Pause for a few moments of silence.]

GOSPEL READING: [A continuation of the above reading.]
Reader: Now his parents went to Jerusalem every year at the feast of Passover. And when he was twelve years old, they went up according to custom; and when the feast was ended, as they were returning, the boy Jesus stayed behind in Jerusalem without his parents knowing it. They assumed he was with the caravan and it was only after a day's journey that they began to look for him among the relatives and acquaintances; and when they did not find him, they returned to Jerusalem, seeking him.

After three days, they found him in the temple, sitting among the teachers listening to them and asking them questions; and all who heard him were amazed at his understanding and his replies. They were astonished when they saw him; and his mother said to him, "Son, why have you done this to us? Your father and I have been worried, looking for you." And he said to them, "Why were you looking for me? Did you not know I must be busy with my father's affairs?" But they did not understand what he meant. He then went down with them and came to Nazareth and was obedient to them.

. . . And Jesus increased in wisdom and in stature and in favor with God and humanity. And his mother kept all these things in her heart. . . .

[Pause again for a few moments of silence.]

[The following may be delivered aloud or read silently.]

Again, Mary "kept all these things in her heart."

Simeon, inspired by the spirit, takes Mary's child into his arms and calls him a Light to The Gentiles and The Glory of Israel. And as Mary and Joseph marvel at what is being said, Simeon adds, "He is set for the fall and the rise of many . . . a sign that will be opposed. . . . And a sword will pierce your soul too, Mary." The shadow of the cross falls early on this family gathered in Jerusalem's temple. Suffering is an inevitable part of the life of one who attempts to "hear the word of God and keep it," a message to be pondered by Luke's community and by disciples of all ages.

The prophetess Anna speaks of this child to all who come to the temple looking for redemption. And when Mary and Joseph and Jesus return to their own home, the child grows quickly as all children do. He becomes strong and wise and enjoys the favor of God. And Mary savors these years as all mothers do; she ponders continually the mystery of his life, and she trusts that God's word will be fulfilled in her Son.

And when he is twelve years old, the age of entry into adulthood, Jesus again journeys with his parents to Jerusalem for Passover. The next time Luke shows Jesus setting foot toward Jerusalem it will be for his final observance of Passover, the one that coincides with his own. On that trip Jesus is also absent for three days before he reappears as the risen Lord.

At his first visit to the temple, the prophets Simeon and Anna, filled with the Holy Spirit, had interpreted the meaning of his life and mission. This time he sits among the prophets and teachers himself and dialogues with them. This time he interprets his own identity and mission for his astonished parents, "Why were you worried? Don't you know my priorities are different now? I am in the house of our God, busy about divine affairs. I must be faithful to my purpose in life." This Jesus, son of Mary is also uniquely son of God. The Jesus of Luke's infancy narrative is growing into his mission. The full understanding of his identity and mission will come only after that final Passover when he reappears as risen Lord. For now Mary and Joseph must be content to allow him the freedom to grow in wisdom as well as stature, in age and in grace.

And his mother "kept all these things in her heart," knowing that his family, his mother and sister and brother, are those who "hear the word of God and keep it"(cf. Luke 8:21).

[Pause for a few moments of silent reflection.]

DISCUSSION/REFLECTION:
What experiences, insights, or feelings can you share that might be similar to those Mary must have encountered during the infancy and childhood of her son?

CLOSING SONG: Sing together a Christmas carol or other appropriate hymn.

THE FEAST OF EPIPHANY

PRAYER SERVICE FOR THE FEAST OF EPIPHANY

THEME: Manifestation and Fulfillment

GATHERING RITUAL: Gather in a space with Christmas decorations, including a manger scene with Magi and gifts, perhaps around a fireplace. There should be incense burning and one large lighted candle on a table.

FOCUS TIME: A moment of silence followed by singing a Christmas carol, such as "We Three Kings."

Leader: The light shines on in darkness.
All: THE LIGHT SHINES IN DARKNESS.
Leader: Rise up in splendor, Jerusalem!
   Your light has come,
     the glory of God shines on you.
   See, darkness covers the earth,
     and thick clouds the people;
   But on you our God shines,
     and over you appears God's glory.
   Nations shall walk by your light
     and kings by your shining radiance
         (cf. Isaiah 60:1-6).
All: THE LIGHT SHINES IN DARKNESS.
Leader: Raise your eyes and look about;
    they all gather and come to you.
   Your sons come from afar,
     and your daughters as well.
   Then you shall be radiant at what you see;
     your heart shall throb and overflow.
   For the riches of the sea
     shall be emptied out before you;
   The wealth of nations shall be brought to you.

All: THE LIGHT SHINES IN DARKNESS.
Leader: Caravans of camels shall fill you,
                 dromedaries from Midian and Ephah;
        All from Sheba shall come,
                 bearing gold and frankincense,
        And proclaiming the praises of God.
All: THE LIGHT SHINES IN DARKNESS.

GOSPEL READING: [cf. Matthew 2:1-12]

Reader 1:

Astrologers from the east arrived one day in Jerusalem inquiring, "Where is the newborn King of the Jews? We observed his star at its rising and have come to pay him homage." At this news King Herod became greatly disturbed and all Jerusalem with him. Summoning the chief priests and scribes, he inquired of them where the Messiah was to be born. "In Bethlehem of Judea," they informed him. "Here is what the prophet has written:

> And you, Bethlehem, land of Judah, are by no means least among the princes of Judah, since from you shall come a ruler who is to shepherd my people Israel."

Herod called the astrologers aside and found out from them the exact time of the star's appearance. Then he sent them to Bethlehem, instructing them, "Report your findings to me so that I too may go and offer him homage."

Reader 2:

As they set out, the star which they had seen at its rising went ahead of them until it came to a standstill over the place where the child was. They were overjoyed . . . and, on entering the house, found the child with Mary his mother and they fell down and worshiped him. . . .

[Pause here for a moment of silent homage.]

Reader 3:

Then, opening their treasures, they presented him with gifts of gold, frankincense, and myrrh. And being warned in a dream not to return to Herod, they went back to their own country by another route.

[Sing together (or listen to a recording of) an appropriate Christmas carol, such as "We Three Kings" or "O Little Town of Bethlehem."]

[The following may be delivered aloud or read silently.]

"On entering the house, they found the child
with Mary his mother. And they fell down
and worshiped him."

On the feast of Christmas, both at midnight and at dawn, the Gospel narrative comes from Luke, who dwells lovingly on the babe wrapped in swaddling clothes and the visit of poor Jewish shepherds. Prompted by an appearance of angels, the shepherds "went with haste and found Mary and Joseph and the babe lying in a manger." And Luke adds that "all who heard it wondered, but Mary kept all these things, pondering them in her heart."

On this, the ancient feast of Epiphany, we turn to the account given by Matthew who simply announces that Mary gave birth to a son born at Bethlehem. He then contrasts the response of a faithless Jewish king and his advisors to that of Gentile astrologers from the East, the wealthy and learned Magi, with roots in the ancient priestly caste of Persia (LaVerdiere, *The Year of Luke*, p.34). While Luke's shepherds were startled by a sudden revelation of angels, Matthew's astrologers, sincere searchers of truth, were led by a star which "came to rest over the place where the child was . . . and going into the house they saw the child with Mary, his mother."

These infancy narratives of Matthew and Luke are theo-logical reflections from the perspective of a later generation of Christians. They make use of a Jewish literary technique called *midrash* which weaves together scriptural interpretation with reflection on contemporary events; in this case, basic components of the Gospel tradition are combined with tales and quotations from the Hebrew scripture (Senior, *Invitation to Matthew*, p. 33). The infancy narrative of Matthew portrays the essential message of the Gospel in miniature—that God has made Godself present to us in the life of one who walked on this earth, indeed, so truly present that this one, Jesus, was God's Son. This revelation was an offense and contradiction to some, but salvation to those who had eyes to see. Of the latter, the Magi are truly the forerunners (Brown, *An Adult Christ at Christmas*, p. 14).

Mary's familiarity with the Hebrew scriptures, combined with her deep faith and trust that God's word to her would be fulfilled, must have prompted her also to reflect on "these (contemporary) things" in light of tales and quotations from the Bible. She must have composed her own *midrash* as she remembered her foremothers: Sarah who laughed at God's promise that she would bear a son; Hannah who gave birth to Samuel and whose song seems to have inspired Mary's "Magnificat." She must have experienced also the ongoing support of her contemporary and cousin, Elizabeth, whose son John was the forerunner of the public ministry of Jesus.

Perhaps she recalled outsiders from the past who, like Matthew's Magi, were blessed by God, and whose stories are included in the Hebrew scriptures: Hagar, the slave woman in Genesis 16; Ruth, Tamar, Rahab, Bathsheba, all foreigners who were welcomed and admired as women of influence and integrated by marriage into the Jewish race.

She must have pondered also the writings of the prophets, particularly those we have come to associate with the advent and Christmas season: Zephaniah, whose words to Jerusalem, "Fear not, O Zion, be not discouraged! The Lord your God is in your midst, a mighty savior," are echoed in the greeting of the Angel Gabriel to Mary; the many passages from Isaiah and Jeremiah concerning the Messiah that have since been reinterpreted by Christians and applied to the birth of her son.

Both Luke and Matthew end their infancy narratives with a reference to Nazareth, the home of Mary and Joseph and

Jesus. Matthew adds a citation from "the prophets" whose precise identity in the Hebrew scriptures is not evident.

There he settled in a town called Nazareth. In this way what was said through the prophets was fulfilled:

"He shall be called a Nazorean" (Matthew 2:23**). One possible explanation posited by some scholars brings us full circle in our reflections which began with the First Sunday of Advent.

It may be a free rendition of Isaiah 11:1, "a shoot springs from the stock of Jesse," which would involve a play on words between the Hebrew term for "shoot" (nezir) and the name of Jesus' home city (*Senior, Invitation to Matthew*, p.39).

A shoot *has* sprung from the stock of Jesse. Let us, like Mary, respond in word and deed to this "shoot" which is the manifestation of God in our midst. Let us, like Mary, continue to ponder the meaning of these things, keeping them in our hearts. Let us, like Mary, begin to compose our own *midrash* through an artful combination of the Gospel message with its manifestation and meaning in our own lives.

[Pause for a few moments of silent reflection.]

DISCUSSION/REFLECTION:

What is the meaning of "these things" for our own lives and times?

CLOSING SONG: Sing together "We Three Kings" or another appropriate carol.

This could be followed by an exchange of gifts and light refreshments. Participants might also be encouraged to write their own *midrash* to be shared at a later meeting.

THE SEASON OF LENT

The root of the English word used to name this season of the liturgical year is *lente* or springtime. Springtime is nature's season of new beginnings, of reawakening. It is the season when hidden roots begin to stir from their deep winter sleep and to stretch out toward the sun, eventually springing forth with new life. Each year, in late winter/early spring while the weather is still very cold and the skies are winter gray, Christians reach deep into their personal and communal depths to begin an intense period of reflection and renewal. The season of Lent is for us a time of opportunity, a time to bring to light the roots and progress of our relationship with God, a time to reflect together and to encourage one another as we journey toward the celebration of new life at Easter.

Our Lenten observance takes its cue from that for which it prepares: the celebration of the Easter Triduum. In all three Cycles, the lectionary readings for the Sundays of Lent follow a similar structure and theme. The first two weeks with their themes of struggle and theophany parallel the themes of the final (Passion) Sunday and Easter. In the Gospels for the third, fourth, and fifth Sundays of each cycle, we meet various characters in dialogue with Jesus. We are invited to enter the dialogue ourselves, to examine our own lives in light of the example and teaching of Jesus.

In the person of Jesus, we are invited to journey from winter to spring, from Lent to Easter, from death to life.

FIRST WEEK OF LENT

The Gospel reading for the first Sunday in all three Cycles of the Lenten lectionary recounts of the temptation of Jesus. The reading from Mark (Cycle B) is short, simple, and stark, written with the sense of urgency that permeates all of Mark's Gospel:

> At once the Spirit drove him out into the desert, and he remained in the desert for forty days, tempted by Satan. He was among wild beasts, and the angels ministered to him (Mark 1:12,13*).

Mark's account leaves much to the imagination and reflection of the reader. Assuming (as most scripture scholars do) that Mark was the first of the Gospels to be put into writing, the early Christian communities, including those of Matthew and Luke, must have relied upon their own experience and imagination in addition to Mark's Gospel and a common oral or written tradition for their interpretation and description of the temptation.

All three accounts follow chronologically the narrative of the baptism of Jesus with the voice from heaven saying, "You are my beloved Son." All three say that Jesus was led by the Spirit into the wilderness where he spent forty days, a reference to the Israelite's forty years of wandering and murmuring in the desert wilderness. Here Jesus, the New Israel and model for the Gospel communities, would also be put to the test. Unlike the children of God in ages past, this unique Son of God remains steadfast, quoting the Book of Deuteronomy (chapters 6-8) where Moses reminds God's people of their Covenant and of the faithfulness this requires.

While Matthew (Cycle A) and Luke (Cycle C) place the specific temptations in different order, the context of all three versions is the identity of Jesus as Son of God, "You are my beloved Son." Unlike Mark, Matthew and Luke speculate on the content of the temptation, "If you are the Son of God . . ." (cf. Matthew 4:3; Luke 4:3). The first temptation described in both Gospels, to turn stone into bread, has been interpreted in economic or material terms, as the desire to use God's gifts for selfish purposes. But this Son of God is also fully human. He will not circumvent the human condition. To the tempter, Jesus replies, "[We] shall not live by bread alone" (cf. Deuteronomy 6:13).

The second temptation in Matthew (third in Luke) is a challenge to God's providence. "If you are the Son of God, throw yourself down." But Jesus again answers in the words of Deuteronomy, "You shall not tempt the Lord your God" (cf. Deuteronomy 6:16). In the remaining temptation, Jesus is offered all the kingdoms of the world with their power and glory if only he will kneel down in worship of the devil. Once again Jesus reverses expectations. He is not interested in political power or prestige. "You shall worship the Lord your God and [God] only shall you serve."

In the pages that follow, the reader is asked to reflect upon her own experience and that of her contemporary Christian community in light of these passages which have been used for reflection and prayer by generations of Christians.

PRAYER SERVICE FOR THE FIRST WEEK OF LENT

THEME: Identity—This unique Child of God is also the Child of Humanity.

GATHERING RITUAL: As in the season of Advent, come together in a dimly lighted room. Suggested symbols for the season: the color purple; the cross; ashes. (Symbols and environment should remain basically the same for each week of Lent.)

FOCUS TIME: A moment of silence accompanied by background music; could be followed by a Lenten song such as "These Forty Days of Lent."

Leader: Your ways, O God, are love and truth (cf. responsorial refrain, Cycle B).

All: YOUR WAYS, O GOD, ARE LOVE AND TRUTH.

Reader 1: Your ways, O God, make known to me; teach me
your paths. Guide me in your truth and teach me for
you are God, my Savior.

All: YOUR WAYS, O GOD, ARE LOVE AND TRUTH.

Reader 2: Test me, God, and probe me, put me to the trial,
mind and heart; for your steadfast love is before my
eyes and I walk in faithfulness to you.

All: YOUR WAYS, O GOD, ARE LOVE AND TRUTH.

Reader 3: Your ways, O God, make known to me; teach me
your paths. Guide me in your truth and teach me, for
you are God, my Savior.

All: YOUR WAYS, O GOD, ARE LOVE AND TRUTH.

GOSPEL READING: [Candle is lighted; read Mark 1:12-15.]
The Spirit immediately drove Jesus out into the
wilderness. And he was in the wilderness forty days,
tempted by Satan; and he was with the wild beasts;
and the angels ministered to him.

Now after John was arrested, Jesus came into
Galilee, preaching the gospel of God, and saying, "The
time is fulfilled, and the reign of God is at hand; repent
and believe in the Gospel" (cf. Mark 1:12-15; Cycle B).

[Pause here for a few moments of silence.]
[The following may be delivered aloud or read silently.]

Mark's account of the temptation of Jesus, like all of
Mark's Gospel, is short, stark, and direct. It simply reports the
event without editorial comment.

Immediately following the baptism of Jesus, after the
descent of the Spirit and the voice from heaven had established the identity of Jesus as Son of God, and just previous to
the beginning of the public ministry, the Spirit "drove Jesus
into the wilderness," the traditional stomping grounds of evil
spirits, where this divine identity was challenged.

Each evangelist preaches and writes with a particular theological perspective and a particular community of faith in
mind. While Matthew and Luke describe the content of the
temptation, Mark leaves the details open for interpretation
and to the imagination of his own community and of each
generation of Christians. The choice of the reading from Mark
for our reflection allows us to fill in the particulars with
examples from our own experience.

Jesus, with that voice from heaven heavy on his mind,
went into the wilderness. And there he struggled with the
issue of his identity. Who am I? What is the meaning of these
events? What kind of "child of God" am I?

Clearly, this child of God is also child of humanity. The
Greek word used for "tempted" implies "trial, tribulation,
test" (Harrington, MARK, p.8). The temptation of Jesus repre-
sents the struggle of humanity with the powers of evil. And
Jesus, in overcoming the challenge to selfish demonstration of
his divinity, accepts the limitations of the human condition. In
coming to grips with his identity, Jesus rejects whatever
would stand in the way of his humanity and his mission. He
has readied himself for the preaching of the Gospel.

Each of us at one time or another struggles with the issue
of identity. Most of us have asked ourselves these or similar
questions: Who am I? What is the meaning of the particular
events in my life? What kind of child of God am I? What is
the purpose of my existence? What does it mean to be
human?

To be fully human means to know oneself as created in
the image of God and to use one's gifts as intended by God.
Sin involves the misuse of the gifts of God. For Matthew and
Luke, the basic temptation was to power and prestige, to use
the gifts of God for selfish endeavors, to reject the limits of
the human condition, to desire to become like God. As with
the sin of our first parents, this desire to become like God has
been attributed to pride, the capital sin which is traditionally
considered to be the root of all other sin.

However, virtue is not simply the opposite of sinfulness;
virtue lies in the middle. The other extreme, refusing to

acknowledge the goodness and giftedness of the human person as created in the image of God, is equally sinful. For many women, the basic sin is a false humility. They have permitted themselves to be socialized into doubting their own potential, hiding their gifts "under a bushel," and therefore denying to the human community their special feminine insights and much-needed contributions to society. They have doubted their own power and turned it over to others. Conversion will require casting off self-doubt and self-hatred, assuming full responsibility for themselves and equal partnership with men in the transformation of society (Osiek, p. 49).

The response of Jesus to temptation serves as a model for us. We, like Jesus, are both children of God and children of humanity. We, like Jesus, must come to grips with our particular identity and our special gifts; we must reject whatever stands between us and the full development of our potential. We, like Jesus, must grow in understanding both the limits of our humanity and the potential of our divinely bestowed gifts.

[Pause for silent response.]

DISCUSSION/REFLECTION:

How do you imagine the temptation of Jesus?

Do you agree that a common temptation for women has been to doubt their own potential?

How would you describe the basic human temptation?

CLOSING PRAYER: (Adapted from alternative opening prayer, First Sunday.)

Leader: Let us pray at the beginning of Lent for the spirit of repentance.

Reader 1: O God, you formed us from the clay of the earth and breathed into us the spirit of life.

All: YOUR WAYS, O GOD, ARE LOVE AND TRUTH.

Reader 2: But we turned from your face and sinned. Bring us back to you and to the life your Son won for us.

All: YOUR WAYS, O GOD, ARE LOVE AND TRUTH.

Reader 3: Through our observance of Lent, help us to understand the meaning of the life, death, and resurrection of Jesus and teach us to reflect it in our lives.

All: YOUR WAYS, O GOD, ARE LOVE AND TRUTH.

CLOSING SONG: Lenten song as at opening, or instrumental music.

[Participants could write on a piece of paper
a resolution for the weeks of Lent.]

SECOND WEEK OF LENT

As mentioned above, the Gospel readings for the first and second Sundays of Lent foreshadow the themes of Passion Sunday and Easter: temptation and transfiguration, struggle and theophany, faithfulness and resurrection. In all three Synoptic Gospels, the story of the Transfiguration of Jesus, which is the Gospel for the Second week of Lent in all three liturgical cycles, is preceded by a passage on the conditions of discipleship, "If you would come after me, you must deny yourself, take up your cross, and follow me" (cf. Matthew 16:24; Mark 8:34; Luke 9:23). The identity and mission of those who would be disciples is modeled on that of Jesus. In fact, the fate of the disciple is the same as that of the Leader. "Whoever would save your life will lose it and whoever loses your life for my sake will save it" (cf. Matthew 16: 25; Mark 8:35; Luke 9:24).

However, the cross cannot be divorced from the resurrection. Approximately one week later, Jesus invited chosen disciples to come with him to the top of a high mountain, traditional meeting place with deity, where he was transfigured before them. It was a happy moment, a brief moment, an anticipated glimpse of the glory of resurrection. It served as confirmation and reminder of the identity of Jesus as proclaimed at his Baptism by the voice from heaven. Once again, a voice from a cloud proclaims, "This is my beloved Son." This time an admonition is added, "Listen to him" (cf. Matthew 17:5; Mark 9:7; Luke 9:35).

PRAYER SERVICE FOR THE SECOND WEEK OF LENT

THEME: Identity—this Human One is also Divine, the Chosen One of God.

GATHERING RITUAL: Come together in a setting similar to that of Week 1, using the same Lenten symbols: cross, ashes, color purple.

FOCUS TIME: A moment of silence accompanied by background music; this could be followed by a Lenten hymn.

Leader: O God of Light, fullness of life and fountain of truth, in this season of Lent, open our hearts to the voice of your Word and free us from the original darkness that shadows our vision. Restore our sight that we may look upon the vision of your glory, which calls us to repentance and a change of heart (adapted from alternative opening prayer, Second Sunday of Lent).

All: YOUR WAYS, O GOD, ARE LOVE AND TRUTH.

GOSPEL READING: [Candle is lighted, read Luke 9:28-36.]

Jesus took Peter, James, and John [representative disciples] and went up onto a mountain to pray. While he was praying, his face changed in appearance and his clothes became dazzling white. Suddenly Moses and Elijah appeared in glory and spoke of his departure which he was to accomplish in Jerusalem. Now those who were with him had fallen into a deep sleep; on awakening, they saw his glory and the two who stood with him. When these were leaving, Peter said to Jesus, "How good it is for us to be here! Let us set up three booths, one for you, one for Moses, and one for Elijah," not knowing what he was saying. While he was speaking, a cloud came and overshadowed them, and they were afraid. Then from the cloud came a voice which said, "This is my Son, my Chosen One. Listen to him." When the voice fell silent, Jesus was there alone. The disciples kept silence and told no one in those days what they had seen (cf. Cycle C).

[Pause here for a few moments of silence.]
[The following may be delivered aloud or read silently.]

What happened on the mountain top? A vision? A disclosure? A religious experience? What is the purpose of this happening recorded in all three Synoptic Gospels? How did it affect the disciples who experienced it? How did it affect the early community? How does it affect us?

In the Christian tradition, the disciples who accompanied Jesus to the mountain top have been remembered as members of the inner circle of friends and disciples of Jesus. Peter is the traditional spokesperson and leader of "the twelve." For our purposes here, let us think of these three as representative disciples. They represent "the twelve" as well as others who follow Jesus. Contemporary male disciples may identify with Peter or one of the sons of Zebedee or Peter's brother Andrew or another member of "the twelve." Women will identify more readily with one of the many Marys or with Johanna, or Susanna or Martha or some of the other women disciples who followed Jesus along the way. (See, for example, Luke 8, the chapter immediately preceding the story of the Transfiguration.) The women disciples are rarely included in the lectionary readings and, until recently, have been over-looked by biblical scholars as well as spiritual writers and preachers.

Clearly, the disciples who followed Jesus to the mountain top were visited by God. They had a religious experience which words cannot describe. They did not know what to say. The extroverted one, the impetuous one had to say some-thing, but we are told he "did not really know what he was saying." Eventually all of them came to the only appropriate response: silence. They must have "pondered these things in their hearts" even as Mary, the mother of Jesus, pondered the many things she had experienced in her own heart.

Religious experience takes place in human settings. The heavenly voice had spoken to Jesus at his baptism and the human Jesus wanted to share that experience with his close friends. He had invited them to become a part of his life and his mission, and he wanted to be known and understood by them. So he took them apart and shared with them his limit-ed understanding of his identity and his mission. It was a human and personal disclosure that took place in a moment of prayer. It was a moment in time, but it involved the past (Moses and Elijah, representing the Law and the Prophets) and the future (mention of his departure or exodus, a reference to the Passion and Death). It was a moment on a mountain top, an earthly setting, but it was a moment when the heavens opened, when the majesty and glory of God were visibly present in Jesus a foreshadowing of the glory of Resurrection. The words, "This is my Son, the Chosen One" are supported by the vision of Jesus in glory, his face radiant and his countenance dazzling white. It was a moment of inspiration and insight for the disciples, a confirmation of the Chosen One. It was confirmation also of his earlier words about discipleship, "If you want to be a disciple of mine, you must . . . take up your cross daily and follow me." It was also a promise that the cross is not the end of the journey.

Each of us has experienced such moments of revelation and inspiration, whether in one of those *ahah!* moments when we seem to receive a sudden and unsolicited inspiration or at times set apart. Lent is a season set apart for Christians to focus on the meaning of discipleship. To be a disciple means not only to follow Jesus, but to be in relationship with him, to share not only in his mission, but in his thoughts and dreams, to come to know him as friend and confidant, to "listen to him." Tonight (today) we have come apart to pray and to reflect with one another on the meaning of these Lenten readings for us. Let us take a few moments to accompany Jesus to the mountain top, to imagine ourselves in his physical presence and to enter into dialogue with him. How good it is for us to be here!

[Allow extra time for silent reflection. Participants may be encouraged to write out their reflection or to take notes (just for themselves).]

DISCUSSION/REFLECTION: [Maintaining an atmosphere of quiet reflection, the leader should offer the opportunity for sharing by those who desire to do so, acknowledging that silence is also an appropriate response.]

CLOSING PRAYER: (Adapted from Psalm 27, Sunday, Cycle C.)
Leader: God is my light and my salvation. Whom should I
        fear?

All: YOUR WAYS, O GOD, ARE LOVE AND TRUTH.

Leader: Your presence, O God, I seek; hide not your face from me.

All: YOUR WAYS, O GOD, ARE LOVE AND TRUTH.

Leader: I believe that I shall see the glory of God in the land of the living. Wait for God with courage; be stouthearted and wait for God.

All: YOUR WAYS, O GOD, ARE LOVE AND TRUTH.

Leader: O God of love and truth, help us to listen to your Son. Enlighten us with your word, that we may find the way to your glory.

All: AMEN.

THIRD WEEK OF LENT

The Gospel readings in Cycle A for the third, fourth, and fifth Sundays of Lent are taken from John. They present Jesus in dialogue with individuals who meet him along the way. The first two meetings, with the Woman of Samaria and the One Born Blind, appear to happen by chance. In the fifth week, Jesus is observed in dialogue with friends in their time of need. The choice of these readings for the Lenten lectionary is intended to apply the Paschal mystery to various aspects of Christian living (Simcoe, ed., *Parish Path through Lent and Eastertime*, p.18).

John's Gospel was written for members of a community struggling to identify themselves in relationship to Jesus and to their world. As the first disciples were confronted and challenged by the presence of the earthly Jesus, so disciples of the evangelist's community and of our own time are confronted and challenged by the same Christ at work through the Spirit in the Christian community. The Fourth Evangelist presents the coming to faith of disciples as a progression in knowledge, love, and commitment achieved in a personal dialogical relationship to Jesus. The characters are paradigmatic of believers/non-believers; each believer is on a continuum of faith/unfaith. Experiential knowledge of Jesus is essential and John expects the believers in his community to deepen their own personal rootedness in Jesus through identification with one or more characters who are presented in the Gospel as models or counter-models of growth in faith. For John, this personal rootedness in Jesus is what creates community, and the community's loving service to one another becomes the means through which the mission of Jesus is continued in the lives of disciples of every age.

Just as the teachings of Jesus and his interaction with others in the Gospels provide us with the only portrait we have of who he is and what he does, so do the writings of a particular Christian community provide us with a glimpse of that community's interpretation of the Jesus tradition. The Gospel of John gives special attention to the interaction of Jesus with certain women. In fact, it is in dialogue with women in the Fourth Gospel that Jesus discloses some of the more important elements of his self-revelation. He leads the Woman of Samaria (John, 4) to call him "Messiah," and he teaches her in symbolic language about the life of grace. He leads Martha of Bethany (John 11) to the ultimate profession of faith (reserved to Peter in the Synoptics). And it is to a woman, Mary of Magdala, (John 20) that he first reveals himself after his own resurrection; he gives to her the commission to announce his victory over death.

PRAYER SERVICE FOR THE THIRD WEEK OF LENT

THEME: Identity—"I Who Speak to You Am He."

GATHERING RITUAL: Come together around a low table with symbols used in the first two weeks plus a water jug.

FOCUS TIME: A moment of silence accompanied by background music; could be followed by a Lenten hymn or other appropriate song.

Leader: Your ways, O God, are love and truth.
All: YOUR WAYS, O GOD, ARE LOVE AND TRUTH.
Leader: As the deer longs for the running waters, so my soul
      longs for you, O God (cf. Psalm 42:2).
All: YOUR WAYS, O GOD, ARE LOVE AND TRUTH.
Leader: Athirst am I for God, the living God. When shall I go
      and behold the face of God (cf. Psalm 42:3)?
All: YOUR WAYS, O GOD, ARE LOVE AND TRUTH.

GOSPEL READING AND REFLECTION: (John 4:5-42) [The following should be read slowly and reflectively.]

Leader: The introduction to the story of the Woman of
      Samaria presents Jesus making his way from Judea
      toward Galilee, deliberately turning away from the

unbelieving Pharisees. The evangelist tells us: "In a city of Samaria, near Jacob's well, . . . Jesus . . . weary from his journey . . . sat down . . . to rest." Jesus is tired and weary and vulnerable. The importance of this episode is underscored by precise indications of time and place (McPolin, p. 41).

Narrator: About the sixth hour . . .

Leader: High noon—not the usual time for drawing water in the heat of the Palestinian sun.

Narrator: Beside the well . . .

Leader: The site of a well is a familiar setting in the Hebrew Scriptures for encounters between women and men which have significance for salvation history.

Narrator: Isaac looking for a wife; Jacob and the daughters of Laban; Moses and the daughters of the priest of Midian.

Leader: John's portrayal of Jesus as "tired and seated" pre- pares us for a very touching and human interaction in the drama that follows. The encounter begins, as rela- tionships usually do in Johannine stories, with the ini- tiative of Jesus. A woman comes to draw water and Jesus says to her:

Jesus: Give me a drink.

Leader: Now, possibilities for communication could not have been more unfavorable; in fact it was forbidden by law for a Jew to speak to a Samaritan and it was also forbidden for a Jewish man to speak to any woman in public. The woman is startled:

Woman: How is it that you, a Jew, ask a drink of me, a woman of Samaria?

Leader: And the evangelist adds,

Narrator: For Jews have no dealings with Samaritans.

Leader: In a society where class distinctions rule over rela- tionships, the only way to relate is in terms of one-up, one-down. The woman identifies herself and Jesus in terms of race and class, but Jesus breaks through those social, religious and political boundaries. He wants to reveal his true identity to this woman of Samaria.

Jesus: If you knew the gift of God and who it is . . . you would have asked him and he would have given you living water.

Leader: The woman does not know who is speaking to her–a familiar motif in John's Gospel—because she is thinking in literal terms. One comes to believe in Jesus only through personal encounter (as with the call of the male disciples in chapter one of John), by the kind of interpersonal relationship offered to this woman by Jesus and symbolically expressed in terms of living water. The dialogue continues, Jesus on the symbolic level and the woman on the natural. Although she does not understand, she remains open and questioning. Relationships of trust require both openness to the other and a willingness to be questioned and challenged.

Woman: You have nothing to draw with . . . where do you get that living water?

Leader: A typical Johannine question about the source of the identity of Jesus (Where do you come from? Where do you live?). A bit of Johannine irony follows:

Woman: Are you greater than our father Jacob who gave us this well?

Leader: The woman taunts him with a challenge and, without realizing it, she has made a true statement about the identity of Jesus. His reply . . .

Jesus: Everyone who drinks this water will thirst again, but whoever drinks of the water that I shall give will never thirst. [It] will become a spring of water, welling up to eternal life.

Leader: . . . includes the claim that Jesus is greater than Jacob. The woman is intrigued but skeptical; her response is ambivalent (sarcastic?):

Woman: Sir, give me this water, that I may not thirst, nor come here to draw . . .

Leader: She does not understand the symbolism. So Jesus switches to the literal level. He challenges the woman with a personal word. On the surface, it looks like an attempt at respectability.

Sandra Louise Litzinger

Jesus: Go, call your husband.

Woman: I have no husband.

Leader: The woman reacts instinctively against his moral probing, but she remains in conversation. Her answer is again ambivalent, even deceptive. Jesus uses the opportunity not to embarrass her, but to invite her to fullness of life.

Jesus: You are right for you have had five husbands, and the one you have now is not your husband.

Leader: Her deeds, her life are exposed. She stands—at high noon—before the light of the world, and the rays of that light enable her to respond,

Woman: Sir, I perceive that you are a prophet.

Leader: At this point the dialogue reaches the crucial moment of judgment, the Johannine moment of decision. The woman has moved hesitantly toward the light. Although she changes the subject to something less personal, she is willing to continue the dialogue.

Woman: Our fathers worshiped on this mountain; and you say in Jerusalem is the place where one ought to worship.

Leader: Jesus begins to speak of a new age when all divisions will cease:

Jesus: When neither on this mountain nor in Jerusalem will you worship the father.

Leader: Worship will not be restricted to one place because its center is the person of Jesus. The woman responds by expressing her hope in a Messiah who would teach them such things. Jesus says to her:

Jesus: I who speak to you am he.

Leader: Jesus entrusts himself to this woman. In dialogical encounter, in personal relationship, she has come to recognize who Jesus is. He accepts the title Messiah from her, although from the religious authorities he never accepts it. (He would not trust himself to them, probably because of the political connotations of messiahship in Judaism.) The dialogue is interrupted here by the approach of the male disciples.

Narrator: They marveled that he was talking with a woman, but none said,

Male Disciple: Why are you talking with her?

Narrator: So the woman left,

Leader: Raymond Brown (*Anchor Bible*, p. 173) suggests that the use of the Greek imperfect tense here, literally . . .

Narrator: They were shocked.

Leader: . . . indicates more than momentary surprise. But their hesitancy to ask questions of Jesus indicates that somehow they knew that they should not be surprised that Jesus would break through the prejudices of his day for the sake of encounter with either a Samaritan or a woman. Meanwhile, backstage,

Narrator: The woman left her water jar.

Leader: . . . the feminine version of fishing nets . . .

Narrator: and went away into the city and said to the people,

Woman: Come, see a man who told me all that I ever did. Can this be the Christ?

Leader: She responds as the male disciples have done in chapter 1 of John's Gospel. She witnesses to others even while she is still in the process of coming to faith.

Narrator: And the Samaritans went out of the city and were coming to him.

Leader: This coming of the Samaritans provides the backdrop for Jesus' dialogue in the following verses with his male disciples. He speaks of fields ripe for the harvest, a reference to the Samaritans coming across the fields to meet him because of the testimony of the woman, a harvest which bears out the saying,

Narrator: One sows and another reaps.

Leader: Jesus continues,

Jesus: I sent you to reap that for which you did not labor; others have labored and you have entered into their labor.

Leader: Clearly, the woman has sown the seed and her apostleship is ratified by Jesus in this dialogue with the male disciples. John describes this woman of Samaria and the male disciples (both at the Last Supper and in the post-resurrection narratives) in identical terminology (Brown, *Community of the Beloved Disciple*, pp. 187-9). As the Triune God sends Jesus, so Jesus sends female as well as male disciples to proclaim the Good News. Both bear witness and both bring others to believe in Jesus on the strength of their word. One comes to faith in Jesus in the Gospel of John only through personal encounter.

In the chance meeting of Jesus with the woman of Samaria, two persons, Jesus and the woman, autonomous and free, yet trusting each other enough to risk violating convention, draw one another into ever deeper dialogue as something of the inner life of each is revealed and spoken to the other. The dialogue itself exposes much about the attitude of Jesus toward ministry in general and toward women in particular. Jesus shows great respect for the person of this woman as he responds to her searching, her intelligence, her ready wit, and her honesty. He approaches her as an equal and encourages her in her own journey, enabling her to move from conventional forms of speech to an inner conviction capable of transforming her life. In conversation with the male disciples, Jesus acknowledges the role of the woman as communicator of the Good News. In his openness, he relates to her life, allowing her to be a catalyst in the process of her own coming to faith. Jesus' ministry to and acceptance of such women must have formed a very important part of his human understanding of his own humanity and of his mission.

[Pause for a few moments of silence.]

DISCUSSION/REFLECTION: [Participants should be invited to share their responses to various aspects of this reflective reading. The following is a possible starter.]

Through her personal encounter with Jesus, the Woman of

Samaria progresses in knowledge, love, and commitment. She becomes a witness and leads others to Jesus even as she is in the process of coming to faith. ("Can he be the Messiah?") As noted in the reflection for the first week of Lent, many women hesitate to use their gifts and talents because of lack of self-confidence. What can we learn from this woman known only as a Samaritan?

CLOSING PRAYER:

Leader: In the spirit of the Woman of Samaria, let us bring our needs before God in openness and gratitude.

[Allow time for spontaneous prayer.]

Leader: O God, Source of love and truth, we ask you to fill us with a portion of that living water you promised, in the person of the Samaritan woman, to those who ask. We seek courage to become, like her, vulnerable in the light of your presence, confident in our ability to proclaim your word, companions with our sisters and brothers through this Lenten season of repentance to the glorious celebration of Easter.

All: AMEN.

FOURTH WEEK OF LENT

The Gospel reading for the fourth Sunday of Lent (Cycle A) continues the presentation of scenarios where Jesus is in dialogue with one who would be a disciple. The setting of this episode is clearly an anachronism. The story of the One Born Blind (John 9:1-41) speaks directly to the situation of the Johannine community at the time the Gospel was written. The atmosphere of hostility, controversy, and division which is personified by the religious authorities reflects the conflict with leaders of the synagogue experienced by Christians near the end of the first century (9:22). The One Born Blind models the experience of the Johannine community, whose lives have been transformed from unbelief, legalism, and blindness to the freedom and conviction of those who have accepted faith in Christ, the light of the world.

The passage begins as a miracle story, but the continuing narrative focuses on the situation of conflict between the forces of light and those of darkness, climaxing in the final confrontation between Jesus, the fullness of light, and the religious leaders who have made their choice for darkness(9:39-41). The One Born Blind comes to faith through gradual acceptance of the light in the person of Jesus; the fundamental sin is deliberate choice of the darkness personified in the religious authorities who harass the One Born Blind and reject Jesus (9:39).

Models and counter-models are presented to the reader in the responses of perplexed neighbors (9:8-12), the unbelieving Pharisees who close themselves off to the light and move into total darkness as the conflict intensifies (9:13-17; 24-34), uncommitted parents who choose not to become involved because they fear the religious authorities (9;18-23), and the One Born Blind who, while continuing to confess ignorance, grows progressively open to the light (9:12,25,36). In the opening lines of chapter nine, John puts on the lips of Jesus the ultimate meaning of the sign and the conflict which follows:

It was not that this blind one sinned nor the parents
but that the works of God might be made manifest. We
must work the works of the one who sent me, while it
is day; night comes when no one can work. As long as
I am in the world, I am the light of the world(cf. 9:3-5).

On one level, the reader witnesses the physical healing of
a blind person; on a deeper level, the witness is to the proclamation of the glory of God that is the work of the Johannine
Jesus. As in the narrative of the Woman of Samaria, the characters in the story remain nameless so that disciples of any
era can more readily identify with the experience of confrontation and challenge, of invitation and response, of acceptance or rejection that characterize the process of coming to
faith and of growth in relationship. It is a story of both progression in insight and regression to total blindness.

PRAYER SERVICE FOR THE FOURTH WEEK OF LENT

THEME: Identity—"I am the light of the world" (9:5).

GATHERING RITUAL: Come together in a dimly lighted room with
Lenten symbols, including an unlighted candle.

FOCUS TIME: A moment of silence accompanied by background
music; this could be followed by a hymn which carries the
theme of light.

Leader: [Candle is lighted.] O God of Light, your ways are
    truth and life.
All: O GOD OF LIGHT, YOUR WAYS ARE TRUTH AND LIFE. Leader: I
    am the Light of the World. The one who follows me
    will have the light of life.
All: O GOD OF LIGHT, YOUR WAYS ARE TRUTH AND LIFE.

GOSPEL READING & REFLECTION: (cf. John 9:1-41)
[This reflective reading could be done by participants before the
group comes together or it could be delivered slowly and reflectively with the group gathered for prayer, perhaps stopping at

appropriate places for quiet reflection and/or discussion. In either case, the scripture passage (John 4:1-41) should be read ahead of time.]

Leader: As he passed by, Jesus "saw" this beggar blind from birth, sitting in darkness (9:1) just as earlier he "saw" Nathaniel sitting under the fig tree(1:48). Jesus sees these future disciples coming to him; he also recognizes their potential for seeing greater things (1:50). So Jesus takes the initiative, commanding the blind beggar,

Reader: Go, wash in the pool of Siloam.

Leader: And the one who was blind came back seeing. Now, the controversy about the sign of healing and the atmosphere of hostility and division that follow illustrate the struggle between the light of faith and the blindness of unbelief. Notice how, throughout the struggle, the one born blind models a kind of assertive behavior that facilitates movement toward the light.

Reader: The neighbors and others acquainted with this beggar asked, "Is this not the one who used to sit and beg?" Some   said, "Yes." Others said, "No." The beggar stated simply, "I am the one." "Then, how were your eyes opened?" they asked. And the one who had been blind replied, "This Jesus made clay and anointed my eyes and said to me, 'Go to the Pool of Siloam and wash.' So I went and washed and received my sight." And they asked, "Where is this Jesus?" "I do not know," replied the beggar born blind (9:9-12).

Leader: The neighbors and others who had known the beggar, divided in their reactions, go to the religious authorities who are also divided in their understanding. In each set of interrogations that follow, the one born blind moves gradually closer to the light in responses that voice an ever-deepening awareness of who Jesus is, while the religious authorities, claiming privileged information about the origin of Jesus and the qualifications of one sent from God (9:16,24,29), move further from the light of truth, preferring the

darkness and security of their conventional understandings. The question about origins dominates this
scene. Some of the Pharisees say,

Reader: "This Jesus is not from God for he does not keep the
Sabbath." But others say, "How can a man who is a
sinner do such signs" (9:16,17)?

Leader: At the very beginning of chapter nine, the reader,
along with "the disciples," had been reminded that
Jesus is the one sent from God (9:4). The Pharisees
now struggle among themselves with the question of
the identity of Jesus. Not satisfied with the answer
the One Born Blind gives to the question,

Reader: "He is a prophet."

Leader: . . . they call in the parents who confirm the condition
of blindness from birth (9:20), but who refuse to comment on the sudden gift of sight (9:21) because:

Reader: They feared the religious authorities who had
already agreed that anyone who should confess Jesus to
be the Christ, was to be put out of the synagogue (9:22).

Leader: At this point, members of John's community are challenged to examine their own progress in faith in the
midst of conflict, and to acknowledge the positive
value of confrontation which fosters growth in insight
and understanding. The Pharisees stand for those
members of the community who close themselves off
to new insights, the legalists, who are satisfied with
answers from past proclamations of dogma and law;
the parents are those caught in the middle, the "fence-
sitters:" "He is of age. Ask him" (9:23). The One Born
Blind models the process of discipleship which
enables growth in faith as one is willing, even in the
midst of conflict and trial, to stand firm in the conviction that arises out of one's own experience of the person of Jesus.

The debate continues as the religious leaders
prod the one born blind to state in the name of God
(9:24) that Jesus is a sinner. But the pressures of these
more searching questions only prompt the One Born

Blind to stand more firmly in the experience of personally knowing Jesus,

Reader: "Why do you want to hear it again? Do you too want to become disciples" (9:27)?

Leader: Finally, the Pharisees attempt to persuade the One Born Blind on the strength of the Mosaic law and the obscurity of the origin of Jesus, "We know that God has spoken to Moses, but as for this Jesus, we do not know where he comes from" (9:29). At this point, the faith of the One Born Blind takes a quantum leap.

Reader: "Why, this is a marvel! You do not know where he comes from, and yet he opened my eyes. . . . Never since the world began has it been heard that anyone opened the eyes of One Born Blind. If this Jesus were not from God, he could do nothing" (9:30-32).

Leader: As the One Born Blind interprets the sign correctly for the unbelieving Pharisees, they continue to bask in the false light of a knowledge that blinds them. (Note the examples of Johannine irony here.) They refuse to open their eyes to the challenge presented by this common and uneducated person born blind whose physical infirmity is for them a sign of inherited sin. Unable to admit their need for light because they "know" (9:31), the Pharisees represent those who are completely closed to ongoing revelation through the Spirit at work in the community.

As the One Born Blind suffers the penalty of excommunication (9:34), Jesus reappears in the story and takes the initiative once again as he brings this new disciple into the full light of faith. Jesus reveals his identity and the One Born Blind recognizes the glory of the manifestation of God in Jesus,

Reader: Jesus . . . found the beggar and said, "Do you believe in the Son of Man?" "Who is he, Sir, that I may believe?" the beggar asks. And the response of Jesus, "You have seen him and it is he who speaks to you," evokes an act of faith, "Lord, I believe!" And this new disciple worshiped Jesus (9:38).

Leader: At this moment, the One Born Blind truly sees. John seems to say here that an unexamined faith is impartial and incomplete. The true identity of Jesus is revealed close up only progressively as the One Born Blind moves toward the light while standing in the experience of conflict and questioning. At first, Jesus is known only as "the one called Jesus" (9:11), then as prophet (9:17), later as one sent from God (9:33); finally, in response to Jesus' own questioning, the One Born Blind is able to recognize the true identity of Jesus and to worship him (9:35-38). The Pharisees, on the other hand, move again further away from the light in their refusal to consider the testimony of anyone who challenges their conventional view of religion. Initially, they seem to accept the healing as miraculous (9:17), then they begin to doubt even the sign as they call in the parents, hoping to show that the blindness never existed at all. By the end, they have lost all interest in finding the truth. Unable to trap the One Born Blind, they pass judgment, "You were born in utter sin, and would you teach us" (9:34)? And they cast this new disciple of Jesus out of the synagogue. Their narrow vision blocks any possibility of openness to the heavenly origin of Jesus.

Finally, Jesus, in the presence of the One Born Blind and of the Pharisees, pronounces his own judgment. He speaks about the division which the full light of his presence provokes. Those who accept the light of faith are able to see beyond the signs; those who choose to reject the one who is the light of the world embrace total blindness. Sin, according to John, is to claim no need for further growth in one's relationship with God in Jesus.

The story of the One Born Blind is intended to encourage the members of the Johannine community whose public witness to faith in Jesus has resulted in their own excommunication from the synagogue and from the social life of the Jewish community. They are encouraged to view conflict as an opportunity, to challenge the status quo wherever and whenever the security of conventional understandings block the light of truth and justice. The beggar born blind models the kind of assertive behavior that allows one to stand firm in conviction born of experience and to hold firm in face of opposition.

The reader is challenged to find self in the drama, identifying with different characters at different moments of faith development. The process of growth is never charted on a straight line, but discipleship is strengthened in conflict. And growth in faith is tied to a willingness to witness to one's present understanding of Jesus, even while continuing to live the questions involved in movement toward the fullness of the light of truth and love. To be rooted in the person of Jesus is to begin to discover the particular shape which that position demands in our day. The light of Christ is constantly at work enlightening the disciple even as it confronts the world. Jesus is the light that is always coming into the world (1:9). Disciples are those who are always responding.

DISCUSSION/REFLECTION:

The leader should offer the opportunity for sharing by those who desire to do so, suggesting that participants identify themselves and their contemporary lives of faith with persons and/or events in the Gospel narrative.

CLOSING PRAYER:

Leader: I am the Light of the World. Those who follow me will have the light of life.

All: I AM THE LIGHT OF THE WORLD, THOSE WHO FOLLOW ME WILL HAVE THE LIGHT OF LIFE.

Leader: O God of Light, fullness of life and fountain of truth, in this season of Lent open our hearts to the voice of your Word and free us from the original darkness that clouds our vision. Restore our sight that we may look upon the vision of your glory which calls us to repentance and a change of heart [adapted from alternative opening prayer, Second Sunday of Lent].

[A hymn which carries the theme of light, such as "I Want to Walk as a Child of the Light" could be sung here.]

FIFTH WEEK OF LENT

In the Gospel reading for the Fifth Sunday of Lent (Cycle A) John continues the dialogical style used throughout his Gospel and exemplified in the stories of the Woman of Samaria and of the Beggar Born Blind. He continues to address situations that are problematic for his community as they strive to live in the light of faith in Jesus and struggle with the synagogue authorities who seem to them to be living in darkness.

In the dialogue with the Woman of Samaria, Jesus had crossed the forbidden boundaries of race and gender to bring the woman into the light (at high noon) and life of grace, affirming her as a person worthy of discipleship and capable of witnessing in a manner that was to bring others to believe in Jesus on the strength of her word. Clearly this woman is seen by John and modeled for the Johannine community as an apostle.

In the story of the Beggar Born Blind, John addressed the traditional Jewish belief that physical infirmity is caused by sin on the part of an individual. In the case of an infirmity from birth, the cause was believed to be sin on the part of the parents. Jesus states clearly that the cause of blindness has nothing to do with individual sin nor the sin of one's parents; rather this blindness would provide the opportunity for the works of God to be manifest. In conversation with Jesus and with various other characters both the Beggar Born Blind and the Woman of Samaria stand simply in the light and truth of their own experience. And Jesus rewards their integrity. In a similar manner in this Sunday's Gospel, John builds on a traditional Jewish belief that the soul remains near the body for three days after death and that there is no hope of revival after that. So, Jesus arrives at Bethany only when it is certain that Lazarus is dead. And when Jesus raises his friend Lazarus from the dead it is for the glory of God and for strengthening of faith among disciples.

This pericope, placed in chapter eleven of the Gospel of John (immediately preceding the account of the anointing of Jesus for burial by Mary, the sister of Lazarus, and the subsequent entry of Jesus into Jerusalem for the final time), is a foreshadowing and preparation for the "hour" of Jesus' own death and resurrection. Even as Lazarus is being raised to life, the enemies of Jesus are plotting to kill him. In fact, this is the "sign" that provokes a meeting of the Sanhedrin (11:45-53) to discuss how they might put Jesus to death. The motif of dying and rising runs throughout the account as it is applied to Lazarus, to Jesus, and to the individual Christian. Likewise, its placement in the lectionary for this last Sunday before the commemoration of the Passion begins serves as a foreshadowing of the annual celebration of the resurrection of Jesus. The raising of Lazarus is a sign of the victory of Jesus over death and a promise of the resurrection of each individual Christian who, like Lazarus' sister Martha, professes faith in Jesus as "the Christ, the Son of God."

Johannine stories are to be interpreted on various levels of meaning. It has been noted by contemporary scholars that John's use of women throughout the Gospel as carriers of the dialogue which manifests the deeper meaning of various passages indicates that women in the Johannine community were held in esteem and regarded as carriers of the Christian message. In this story of the Raising of Lazarus, it is Martha of Bethany who proclaims belief in Jesus as the Christ.

Raymond Brown (*Community of the Beloved Disciple*, p. 190) suggests that this confession of faith on the lips of Martha parallels that of Peter in the Synoptics, e.g., Matthew 16:16, "You are the Christ, the Son of God," and may be a deliberate move on the part of John to give to a woman a role traditionally associated with the leader of the Twelve. According to Brown, this would not be an attempt to deny the ecclesial role of Peter, but to emphasize that the primary Christian category in the Johannine community is discipleship, not ecclesiastical authority. It would also underscore the point that, in this early Christian community, women and men were equal partners in the proclamation of the Gospel.

PRAYER SERVICE FOR THE FIFTH WEEK OF LENT

THEME: Identity: "I am the resurrection and the life" (John 11:25).

GATHERING RITUAL: Gather as in previous weeks of Lent around traditional Lenten symbols.

FOCUS TIME:
[A moment of silence accompanied by background music; could be followed by singing an appropriate hymn.]

Leader: I am the resurrection and the life. Those who believe in me will never die.

All: I AM THE RESURRECTION AND THE LIFE. THOSE WHO BELIEVE IN ME WILL NEVER DIE.

Leader: If the Spirit of the one who raised Jesus from the dead dwells in you, then the one who raised Jesus from the dead will bring your mortal bodies to life also through the Spirit dwelling in you (cf. Romans 8:11; Second reading, Cycle A).

All: I AM THE RESURRECTION AND THE LIFE. THOSE WHO BELIEVE IN ME WILL NEVER DIE.

GOSPEL READING: [Candle is lighted; read John 11:1-45 or the following selected verses.]

The sisters of Lazarus sent word to Jesus, "The one you love is sick." Upon hearing this Jesus said, "This sickness is not to end in death; rather it is for God's glory." Jesus loved Martha and her sister and Lazarus very much.

When Jesus arrived at Bethany, he found that Lazarus had already been in the tomb four days. When Martha heard that Jesus was coming she went out to meet him, while Mary sat at home. Martha said to Jesus, "Lord, if you had been here, my brother would not have died. Even now I am sure that God will give you whatever you ask." "Your brother will rise again," Jesus assured her. "I know he will rise again," Martha replied, "in the resurrection on the last day." Jesus told her: I am the resurrection and the life. Whoever believes in me, though the same should die, will come to life; and whoever is alive and believes in me will never die. Do you believe this? "Yes, Lord," she replied.

"I have come to believe that you are the Christ, the Son of God; the one who is to come into the world."

When she had said this, she went and called her sister Mary, saying quietly, "The Teacher is here and is calling for you." When Jesus saw her weeping, he was deeply moved in spirit and troubled; and he said, "Where have you laid him?" Then Jesus, deeply moved again, came to the tomb; it was a cave and a stone lay upon it. And Jesus lifted up his eyes and said, "Father, I thank you that you have heard me. I know that you hear me always, but I have said this on account of the people standing by, that they may believe that you have sent me." Then Jesus cried with a loud voice, "Lazarus, come out!" The one who was dead came out, bound and wrapped. Jesus said, "Unbind him and let him go free" (cf. John 11:1-4).

[Pause for a few moments of silence.]
[The following could be delivered aloud or read silently.]

On his arrival in Bethany, at the home of his friends Mary (who will later anoint his feet for burial), her sister Martha, and their brother Lazarus, Jesus learns that Lazarus has already been in the tomb four days. Now, the evangelist tells us that Jesus "loved Martha and her sister and Lazarus." Readers of the Gospel of Luke (10:38-42) will recall meeting the sisters Martha and Mary in that Gospel as well when, as in this episode from the Gospel of John, Jesus visits their home in Bethany. Characterizations of the sisters are similar in the two Gospels. In both accounts they are presented as friends of Jesus and in each account one of the sisters enters into a theological discussion led by Jesus. Martha appears as the extrovert, the more active one, while Mary is presented as quieter and more reflective. The love of Jesus for this family is evident in both accounts. These women play important roles in the life of Jesus, not only as friends, but as model disciples and examples of the leadership of women in the early Church.

In the current episode, Martha runs out to greet Jesus while Mary remains in the house with the other guests, "If you had been here, my brother would not have died" (11:21). Martha is conscious of the reputation of Jesus as a miracle worker, but she does not yet understand the significance of his power to give life. She does, however, regard her friend as one whose prayer is heard by God, "And even now I know that whatever you ask from God, God will give you" (11:22).

Jesus builds on Martha's spoken faith in his power to heal to evoke her deeper expression of faith in his person. His response, "Your brother will rise again" (11:23), prompts Martha to articulate belief in the general resurrection. In turn, Jesus claims that he is the resurrection and the life. One must believe in him to come to life. "Do you believe this?" he asks Martha (11:26). Martha responds with a Christological confession of faith, "Yes, Lord, I believe that you are the Christ, the Son of God, the one who is coming into the world" (11:27). Just as Peter's solemn confession of faith at Caesarea Philippi (Matthew 16:16) is praised by Jesus as the proclamation of divine revelation, this identical statement on the lips of Martha comes also in the context of a major revelation of Jesus, a Johannine "I am" statement, "I am the resurrection and the life" (11:25). Martha's later hesitation at the tomb, "Lord, by this time there will be an odor, for he has been dead four days" (11:39), showing that her faith is not yet fully mature, does not weaken the parallelism with Peter. His obtuseness is demonstrated in Matthew immediately after Jesus has conferred upon him what has been interpreted in the Church as the role of primacy (Matthew 16:18,19). When Peter begins to rebuke Jesus for speaking of his approaching suffering and death (Matthew 16:21), Jesus calls him a hindrance. And, very soon, Peter will openly deny Jesus (Matthew 26:69-75).

Just as in the Synoptics Jesus evokes a confession of faith from Peter in a context of conversation, so also in John, Jesus evokes a similar confession of faith from a woman of Bethany, his friend, Martha, in the context of dialogue with her. If Raymond Brown's theory is correct, then John's account of the raising of Lazarus serves not only as a major "sign" of the true identity of Jesus as the Christ, giver of life, and as a pre-figuring of his own resurrection, but also as an indication that in Christ a new relationship between men and women begins. This new relationship opens a dialogue, the purpose of which is to liberate women's gifts and acknowledge their rights (Schelkle, p. 149).

As did the Woman of Samaria, and the Beggar Born Blind, Martha of Bethany enters into a dialogue with Jesus that is staged by John to reveal the true identity of Jesus as light of the world and life of all who believe. Their stories begin and end at various points on the continuum of faith/unfaith, but for all of them, the result is gradual progression in faith through personal encounter with Jesus. As mentioned in the introduction to the season of Lent, these pericopes are chosen for the third, fourth, and fifth Sundays of Lent because they invite us to enter into the dialogue ourselves and to examine our own lives in light of the example of these early disciples and their relationship with Jesus. Let us pause here for a few moments to reflect on the encounter of Martha with Jesus and to enter into the dialogue as Martha stands in relationship to Jesus as her friend and consoler, as teacher, and as the Christ, the resurrection and the life.

[Pause here for a few moments of silence.]

DISCUSSION/REFLECTION: Participants should be invited to share their reflections in dialogue with one of the characters from the Gospel of John as it relates to their own lives or to contemporary people of faith.

CLOSING PRAYER:
Leader: The one who lives and believes in me will not die forever (cf. John 11:26).
All: THE ONE WHO LIVES AND BELIEVES IN ME WILL NOT DIE FOREVER.
Leader: Unless a grain of wheat falls on the ground and dies, it remains a single grain; but if it dies, it yields a rich harvest (cf. John 12:24,25).
All: THE ONE WHO LIVES AND BELIEVES IN ME WILL NOT DIE FOREVER.

CLOSING SONG: An appropriate song should be sung or played; such as "I Am the Resurrection."

HOLY WEEK: THE FEAST OF ANOINTING

Holy Week begins with the Gospel proclamation of Jesus' solemn and final entry into Jerusalem. Traditionally this reading is followed by the procession of palms. The first and second readings as well as the responsorial psalm for the Eucharistic Liturgy for Passion Sunday are the same for all three cycles. The Gospel is the Passion Narrative from one of the Synoptics. On Good Friday, the reading of the Passion is from the Gospel of John.

The first reading for Sunday, Isaiah 50:4-7, is taken from the third song of the Suffering Servant passages. From earliest times, the Christian community has applied these readings to Jesus and, along with Psalm 22, the responsorial psalm, they are used throughout Holy Week as a commentary on the Passion. The second reading for Sunday, Philippians 2:5-11, incorporates an early church hymn which summarizes the Christian belief concerning Jesus from incarnation to resurrection. The reading begins with the admonition, "Your attitude must be Christ's," an appropriate theme for all of Holy Week.

The pages that follow offer two sets of reflections or rituals, beginning with the Gospel for Monday of Holy Week which portrays Mary of Bethany anointing the feet of Jesus. The second section focuses on the passion of Jesus. It presents a collage of readings, taking a special look at the women who, according to all four Gospels, follow Jesus along the way of the cross.

PRAYER SERVICE FOR THE FEAST OF ANOINTING

THEME: Identity—"Truly this was the Son of God" (cf. Mark 15:39).

GATHERING RITUAL: Gather in silence or with appropriate background music, using only a simple wooden cross as symbol and a small bottle of perfumed oil. (The cross could be made from two bare twigs.)

Leader: Here is my servant, my chosen one with whom I am
well pleased, upon whom I have put my spirit.

All: HERE IS MY SERVANT, MY CHOSEN ONE WITH WHOM I AM WELL
PLEASED, UPON WHOM I HAVE PUT MY SPIRIT. (Taken from
Isaiah 42:1-7, First Reading for Monday of Holy
Week).

Leader: My servant shall bring forth justice to the nations, not
crying out, not shouting, not heard in the street. A
bruised reed my servant shall not break; the smoldering wick shall not be quenched until justice is established upon the earth; the coastlands will wait for my
servant's teaching.

All: HERE IS MY SERVANT, MY CHOSEN ONE WITH WHOM I AM WELL
PLEASED, UPON WHOM I HAVE PUT MY SPIRIT.

Leader: Thus says God who created the heavens and
stretched them out. . . . I have called you for the victory of justice, I have grasped you by the hand; I formed
you and set you as a covenant of the people, a light
for the nations.

All: HERE IS MY SERVANT, MY CHOSEN ONE WITH WHOM I AM WELL
PLEASED, UPON WHOM I HAVE PUT MY SPIRIT.

Leader: To open the eyes of the blind, to bring out prisoners
from confinement, and from the dungeon, those who
live in darkness. I am God; this is my name.

All: HERE IS MY SERVANT, MY CHOSEN ONE WITH WHOM I AM WELL
PLEASED, UPON WHOM I HAVE PUT MY SPIRIT.

GOSPEL READING: John 12:1-11; (Mark 14:3-9)

Six days before Passover Jesus came again to Bethany
[the village of his friends Mary and Martha and their
brother] Lazarus whom Jesus had raised from the dead.
They gave a dinner for him there. . . . And Mary took a
liter of costly perfumed oil made from genuine aromatic
nard and anointed the feet of Jesus and dried them with
her hair; the house was filled with the fragrance of the oil.

Then Judas Iscariot, one of his disciples and the one
who would betray him said, "Why was this oil not sold
for three hundred day's wages and given to the poor?" He

said this not because of concern for the poor, but because he was a thief and held the money bag. So Jesus said, "Leave her alone. Let her keep this for the day of my burial. You always have the poor with you, but you do not always have me." And truly I say to you, wherever the Gospel is preached in the whole world, what she has done will be told in memory of her (cf. Mark 14:9).

The [religious authorities] found out he was there and came, not only because of Jesus, but also to see Lazarus whom Jesus had raised from the dead. And the chief priests plotted to kill Lazarus too because many were . . . believing in Jesus because of him (cf. John 12:1-11).

[Pause here for a few moments of silence.]
[The following may be delivered aloud or read silently.]

Six days before Passover, the one who had come to bring good news to the poor, freedom to the oppressed, nourishment to the hungry, and drink to the thirsty accepts hospitality from his friends at Bethany, and the gentle, loving ministry of one for whom he had been the mentor. Mary of Bethany ministers to Jesus. How courageous she was! How gently Jesus receives her love and defends her . . . along with all the poor of the world (Stuhlmueller, *Biblical Meditations for Lent*, p.83).

This Suffering Servant does not cry out or shout as others cry out against him and against his friend Mary who anoints his feet. But Jesus will not permit the ministry of this woman—this pouring out of love that does not count the cost—to be stamped out like a "smoldering wick" (Stuhmueller, above). Mary has performed a symbolic gesture, a prophetic action. Six days before Passover, she calls attention to the death and burial of Jesus. And the Church places this reading on Monday of Holy Week where it serves to keep our attention focused on those same sacred events (MacRae, p. 146).

This anointing is an extravagant action, but ordinary activity is suspended when the death of a loved one is near. Courageous women and men of every age do extravagant things for life and for love. Mary of Bethany has reminded those present at table who it is they have in their midst. And her lavish gesture fills the house at Bethany—and our house—with the fragrance of the ointment.

Jesus sits at table with us. He meets us as we are at this moment. We, like Mary of Bethany, are called to love Christ as he loves us, completely and unreservedly, and to share that kind of love with others. And that is always risky. People may scorn us or laugh at us, or take advantage of us, or worse yet, ignore us, pretend we don't exist. Sometimes our actions cost more than we had planned to give. "Why was this ointment, a whole liter of costly perfume, thus wasted?"

Jesus' defense of the woman confounds his critics. She has not given alms, but her personal act of love for one in need, preparation for burial, is a gesture of equal value. And she has done this act of loving kindness to Jesus. "The poor you will always have with you, . . . but you will not always have me" (Mark 14:7**). Such extravagance makes no sense to Judas. And neither does care for the poor! Love of God and love of the poor are much the same. Commitment to either is always on their terms and not our own.

Let us remember the poor this week; let us also be aware of Mary's sense of timing. We too are preparing for Passover. Let us waste time with Jesus this week and let us not count the cost. Let us sit at table with him. Let us sit at his feet and minister to him. Let us also allow Jesus to minister to us. Let us fill our house with the fragrance of our preparation for his death and burial: ". . . wherever the gospel is proclaimed to the whole world, what she has done will be told in memory of her" (Mark. 14:9**).

[After some time for silent reflection, participants anoint each other in turn, saying quietly:]

All:"THE POOR YOU WILL ALWAYS HAVE WITH YOU, . . . BUT YOU WILL NOT ALWAYS HAVE ME."

[There is no formal ending to the services of Holy Week, rather the time is treated as one extended retreat; participants are invited to remain a moment or so in silent reflection, moving to another room as each one is ready to depart.]

HOLY WEEK: THE FEAST OF THE WAY

The earliest proclamation of the gospel was the news that "Jesus is risen!" This oral proclamation was followed by reports of the passion and death, working back through the public life and ministry of Jesus. Each evangelist retells the gospel story as it has been handed down in his own community of faith and from a particular theological perspective. Mark's, the shortest and starkest, is commonly held by scripture scholars to be the earliest written form of the four canonical Gospels and a source for both Matthew and Luke.

The passion narrative in each Gospel carries a theme that is evident in the Gospel as a whole. One of the themes of Mark's Gospel is discipleship. Discipleship, for Mark, is expressed in the geographic symbolism of the journey from Galilee to Jerusalem. The journey begins with the good times of the opening chapters, the miraculous healings in Galilee, and continues through the chapters which present the teaching of Jesus "on the way" from Galilee to Jerusalem. The Gospel concludes with the events surrounding the Passion, the "way" of the cross, the burial and the empty tomb. The original ending of this Gospel leaves the female followers of Jesus at the empty tomb with the young man in a white garment who directs them to "Go, tell his disciples and Peter that he goes before you to Galilee; there you will see him as he told you" (Mark 16:7).

One constant in all the Gospels seldom treated in commentaries or homilies is that female disciples, like the male disciples, followed Jesus from Galilee, ministered to him, and came up with him to Jerusalem. Unlike the male disciples, however, who (according to Mark 14:50 and Matthew 26:56) "forsook him and fled," these women stood by Jesus. They, unlike Peter who also followed at a distance but denied being a disciple, were recognized by Jesus as they publicly "bewailed and lamented him" along the way of the Passion (Luke 23:27). In the Synoptics, the women at Calvary look on from afar (as women of today are expected to do in many religious traditions); according to John, there were women standing by the cross: ". . . his mother and his mother's sister, Mary the wife of Clopas, and Mary of Magdala" (cf. John 19:25).

The theme of the reflection that follows is that the way of Jesus is the way of the disciple. It means following him from symbolic Galilee to Jerusalem, through the passion and death to the road that leads back to Galilee where "he goes before you" (Mark 16:7). It presents the women who follow Jesus along the way as models of discipleship.

PRAYER SERVICE FOR THE FEAST OF THE WAY

THEME: Identity—"Truly this was the Son of God" (cf. Mark 16:39). The way of Jesus is the way of the disciple.

GATHERING RITUAL: Gather in silence or with appropriate background music, using only a simple wooden cross as symbol. (The cross could be made from two bare twigs.)

Leader: My God, my God, why have you forsaken me?
    (Psalm 22)
All: MY GOD, MY GOD, WHY HAVE YOU FORSAKEN ME?
Leader: All who see me scoff at me; they mock me with part-
    ed lips, they wag their heads: "He relied on God; let
    God deliver him, let God rescue him and love him."
All: MY GOD, MY GOD, WHY HAVE YOU FORSAKEN ME?
Leader: Indeed many dogs surround me, a pack of evildoers
    closes in on me; they have pierced my hands and my
    feet; I can count all my bones.
All: MY GOD, MY GOD, WHY HAVE YOU FORSAKEN ME?
Leader: They divide my garments among them, and for my
    vesture they cast lots. But you, O God, be not far from
    me; O my help hasten to aid me.
All: MY GOD, MY GOD, WHY HAVE YOU FORSAKEN ME?
Leader: I will proclaim your name to all; in the midst of the
    assembly I will praise you: "You who fear, praise God;
    give glory to God."
All: MY GOD, MY GOD, WHY HAVE YOU FORSAKEN ME?

GOSPEL READING: (A collage from all four Gospels.)
[These should be proclaimed slowly and reflectively; appropriate background music might accompany the readings; in place of the longer pauses, appropriate hymns known to the participants might be sung or a sung refrain might be repeated each time.]

Reader 1: If any of you would come after me, you must deny yourself, take up your cross, and follow me (cf. Mark 8:34, Luke 9:23, Matthew 16:24). [Brief Pause]

Reader 2: He journeyed through the cities and villages (of Galilee), preaching and proclaiming the good news of the reign of God. The Twelve were with him and also some women . . . Mary called Magdalene, . . . and Joanna, . . . Susanna, and many others who provided for them out of their means (cf. Luke 8:1-3). [Longer Pause]

Reader 1: Behold, we are going up to Jerusalem; and the Son of Humanity will be delivered to the chief priests and the scribes, and they will condemn him to death ... and after three days, he will rise (cf. Mark 10:33, 34). [Brief Pause]

Reader 2: And as they led him away, they seized one Simon of Cyrene, . . . and laid on him the cross to carry it behind Jesus. And there followed him a great multitude, including many women who lamented him and mourned. Jesus turned to them and said, "Daughters of Jerusalem, do not weep for me; weep instead for yourselves and for your children. . . ." (cf. Luke 23:26-28). [Longer Pause]

Reader 1: And when they had sung a hymn they went out to the Mount of Olives. And Jesus said to them, "You will all fall away; . . . But after I am raised up, I will go before you to Galilee. Peter said to him, "Even though they all fall away, I will not." . . . And they all said the same (cf. Mark 14:26-31). [Brief Pause]

Reader 3: And while he was still speaking, Judas came, one of the Twelve, and with him a crowd with swords and clubs. . . . And when he came, he went up to Jesus at once and said, "Master!" And he kissed him. And they laid hands on him and seized him . . . (cf. Mark 14:43-46). [Brief Pause]

Reader 4: And they all forsook him and fled (cf. Mark 14:50). [Longer Pause]

Reader 1: I am the good shepherd and I know mine and mine know me, . . . and I will lay down my life for the sheep. I have power to lay it down and power to take it up again (cf. John 10:14,17,18). [Brief Pause]

Reader 3: His sheep hear his voice as he calls his own by name and leads them out . . . he walks ahead of them and the sheep follow him (cf. John 10:3,4). [Brief Pause]

Reader 2: Standing by the cross of Jesus were his mother and his mother's sister, Mary, the wife of Clopas, and Mary of Magdala. When Jesus saw his mother and the disciple there whom he loved, he said to his mother, "Woman, behold your son." Then he said to the disciple, "Behold your mother." And from that hour the disciple took her into his home (cf. John 19:25-27). [Longer Pause]

Reader 1: If you do not bear your own cross and follow me, you cannot be my disciple (cf. Luke 14:27). [Brief Pause]

Reader 2: There were also women looking on from afar, among whom were Mary Magdalene and Mary the mother of James the younger and of Joses and Salome who, when he was in Galilee, followed him, and ministered to him; and also many other women who came up with him to Jerusalem (cf. Mark 15:40,41). [Longer Pause]

Reader 1: And at the ninth hour Jesus cried with a loud voice, "Eloi, Eloi, lama sabachthani?" which means, "My God, my God, why have you forsaken me?" [Brief Pause]

Reader 2: And Jesus uttered a loud cry and breathed his last (cf. Mark 15:34, 37). [Longer Pause]

Reader 3: And the curtain of the temple was torn in two from top to bottom. And when the centurion who stood facing him saw the manner in which he breathed his last, he said,

Reader 4: "Truly, this was the Son of God." [Longer Pause]

All: Sing "Were You There When They Crucified My Lord?" or another appropriate hymn known to participants.

[There is no formal ending to the services of Holy Week, rather the time is treated as one extended retreat; participants are invited to continue for a while in personal prayer and then move to another room as each one is ready to end the reflection time.]

THE SEASON OF EASTER

Following the penitential season of Lent, we enter into the "glorious Fifty Days, the Great Sunday (seven weeks of seven days), characterized by Easter alleluias, feasting and celebrating . . ." (Bernstein, *Parish Path through Lent and Eastertime*, edited by Mary Ann Simcoe, p.67). In this season we celebrate the life of the risen Christ and reflect on its meaning for us and for the Christian community. In the Lenten readings, as we focused on the interaction of the historical Jesus with his disciples, we included ourselves in the dialogue; in this Easter season, we focus on the risen Christ as the first disciples encountered his presence "on the third day" and in the weeks immediately following the events of his death and burial. Again, we invite ourselves into the setting, this time with a greater sense of wonder and awe, in a spirit more reflective than dialogical. We embrace the mystery of the resurrection of Jesus and its implications for all of us.

The Gospel readings for the Easter season are taken mostly from John, and the first reading for all seven Sundays is from the Book of Acts. The second reading varies from cycle to cycle. All invite us to reflect on the experience of the early Christian community as it comes to grips with daily living in the post-resurrection period, a time of crisis when they could no longer depend upon the physical presence of Jesus, when they learned to live in the Spirit of Jesus as we are called to live in that same Spirit today.

There are various versions in the four Gospels of the Resurrection appearances, just as there are various versions of the Passion and Crucifixion and of the scene at the empty tomb. As noted earlier, one constant in all the Gospels seldom mentioned in commentaries or homilies is that female disciples, like the male disciples, followed Jesus from Galilee, ministered to him, and came up with him to Jerusalem. The women were present also with Joseph of Arimathea when the body of Jesus was laid in the tomb, and they returned on the first day of the week with spices and perfumed oils to anoint his body.

92

For their faithfulness, these women were rewarded with the first appearances of the risen Christ. They became the first Christian witnesses, the apostles to "the twelve." As Peter is named first in lists of the male disciples who became known as "the twelve," so Mary of Magdala is frequently named first among the women disciples who followed Jesus, supported him out of their means, and became the first witnesses to the resurrection. Some early traditions name Mary of Magdala as a leader among the early Christians.

EASTER WEEK: RESURRECTION!

The prescribed readings for Easter Sunday are the same in all three cycles, although an alternative Gospel is provided for each cycle and there is a choice of second readings. The first reading, from chapter ten of Acts, is a summary of Christian preaching about Christ and is directed to Gentiles. In its original setting in Acts, it is delivered to the household of Cornelius, a Roman centurion, "religious and god-fearing," who had been the recipient of a vision in which he saw a messenger of God who told him to send some representatives to Joppa (where Peter had raised Dorcas to life in the previous chapter).

The Gospel for Easter Sunday is the story of the women disciples who go out "very early in the morning on the first day of the week" to anoint the body of Jesus. The account from John's Gospel or a suggested alternate from one of the synoptics may be used in any cycle. Although the particulars differ according to the theological intention of each evangelist, the story line is the same. A collage of readings from the synoptics will be used in the reflection that follows.

PRAYER SERVICE FOR THE FIRST WEEK OF EASTER

THEME: Resurrection!

GATHERING RITUAL: Come together in a brightly lighted and joyfully decorated room with a large white candle burning and with music playing. Suggestion: Handel's "Hallelujah Chorus."

FOCUS TIME: [Join in singing the "Hallelujah Chorus" or another "Alleluia" song.]

Leader: Jesus is risen, Alleluia!
All: JESUS IS RISEN, ALLELUIA!
Leader: This is the day our God has made. Let us rejoice and be glad.
All: JESUS IS RISEN, ALLELUIA!

Sandra Louise Litzinger

GOSPEL READING: [From the Book of Acts.]

Reader 1: Peter proceeded to speak [to them]: "You know . . . , what has happened all over Judea, beginning in Galilee . . . , how God anointed Jesus of Nazareth with the holy Spirit and power. He went about doing good . . . for God was with him. We are witnesses of all that he did both in the country of the Jews and [in] Jerusalem. They put him to death by hanging him on a tree. This man God raised[on] the third day and granted that he be visible, not to all the people, but to us, the witnesses chosen by God in advance, who ate and drank with him after he rose from the dead. He commissioned us to preach . . . and testify that he is the one appointed by God . . . . To him all the prophets bear witness, that everyone who believes in him will receive forgiveness of sins through his name" (Acts 10:34, 37-43*).

All: JESUS IS RISEN, ALLELUIA! [Or sing an "alleluia" song.]
[Pause for a moment of silent reflection.]

Reader 2: A Collage of Readings from the Synoptic Gospels (cf. Luke 24:1-12, Mark 6:1-8, Matthew 28:1-10). And when the Sabbath was over, some of the women who had followed Jesus, including Mary of Magdala, Mary the mother of James and Joseph, the mother of the sons of Zebedee, Joanna and Salome, bought perfumed oil and spices so that they might go and anoint the body of Jesus. And very early on the first day of the week they went to the tomb when the sun had risen. And they were saying to one another, "Who will roll away the stone for us from the door of the tomb?" And looking up, they saw that the stone was rolled back–it was very large.

Entering the tomb, they saw an angel. And they were amazed. The angel said to them, "Do not be amazed. You seek Jesus of Nazareth who was crucified. He has risen; he is not here. See the place where they laid him. Go quickly and tell his other disciples that he is going before you to Galilee; there you will see him."

So they departed quickly with fear and great joy and ran to tell the male disciples. And behold, Jesus met the women on the way and said, "Hail!" And they came up and took hold of him and worshiped him. Then Jesus said to them, "Do not be afraid; go and tell the others to go to Galilee, and there they will see me." And on their arrival, the women told all this to the male disciples but these words seemed to them like an idle tale and they did not believe the women.

[Pause here for a few moments of silence.]
[The following may be delivered aloud or read silently.]

In the first reading from Luke (The Book of Acts), Peter, the witness and spokesperson for the early Christian community, speaks with utter conviction and from his personal experience. We know from other sources, however, including the Gospel of Luke, that Peter himself and the other male disciples were not easily convinced. They were skeptical of the reported experience of others, ". . . these words seemed to them an idle tale, and they did not believe [the women]" (Luke 24:11). Some manuscripts add verse 12, "But Peter rose and ran to the tomb; stooping and looking in, he saw the linen cloths by themselves; and he went home wondering what had happened" (Throckmorton, p.188).

What is the significance of the empty tomb? The women were frightened and amazed by the empty tomb. Peter wondered. The empty tomb is not proof of the resurrection. Easter faith comes from first-hand experience of the Risen Christ. It is pure gift. For the women in Matthew's Gospel, the experience was an appearance of Jesus coming to meet them as they ran away from the empty tomb; for "the eleven" it was an appearance on a mountain in Galilee. In Luke, the masterful story-teller, Jesus becomes present in the person of a traveler on the road to Emmaus and in the breaking of bread.

How do we know that Jesus is risen? Where do we encounter him? Like the travelers to Emmaus, we meet him in our everyday encounters with contemporary Christians, in our companions on the way, in the breaking of bread, whenever two or three of us are gathered in his name. In the words of the late James Dunning, "If you want to know if Jesus is risen, go to the Easter Vigil and look around you!"

[Pause for silent response.]

DISCUSSION/REFLECTION: Respond to the quote from Dunning, "If you want to know if Jesus is risen, go to the Easter Vigil and look around you."

Is it practical advice? Where do we find the risen Christ? Action: Make a conscious effort this week to find good news in places where you least expect it.

CLOSING PRAYER:
Leader: Jesus is risen, Alleluia!
All: JESUS IS RISEN, ALLELUIA!
Leader: This is the day our God has made. Let us rejoice and
        be glad.
All: JESUS IS RISEN, ALLELUIA!

[Repeat Handel's "Hallelujah Chorus" or another "alleluia" song.]

THE SECOND WEEK OF EASTER

The first reading for the Second Sunday of Easter in each cycle is a selection from Acts describing life in the post-resurrection community. The Gospel is the same for all three cycles, John 20:19-31. The Johannine Gospel recommended for Easter Sunday, John 20:1-9, had presented Mary Magdalene's discovery of the empty tomb and her running to tell Peter and the beloved disciple who also ran to the tomb and saw "only the linen cloths lying" (John 20:6). The summarizing statement in verse nine concludes the reading, ". . . for as yet they did not know the scripture, that he must rise from the dead" (20:9).

It seems telling to note that the intervening verses, John 20:10-18, are not included in any Sunday lectionary selections. Verse 10 reads, "Then the [male] disciples went back to their homes." And verses 11, "But Mary stood weeping outside the tomb, . . ." through 18 narrate the appearance of the risen Jesus to Mary who, unlike Peter and the beloved disciple, remains by the tomb contemplating the mysterious events of those very frightening and confusing days.

The assembled Christian community, gathered for liturgy on this Second Sunday of Easter year after year, hears always about the doubting Thomas, but never about the faithful, faith-filled experience of Mary as she encounters the risen Lord outside the tomb. In the lectionary this Gospel is relegated to the liturgy for Easter Tuesday. Is this passage from the Gospel of John, like most other New Testament texts that include the experiences of women, just too much for a male-dominated Christian community to hear, especially since it is placed by the evangelist between two stories of doubting male disciples?

In the reflection that follows, this resurrection narrative from the Gospel of John is proclaimed and the resurrection experience of women is celebrated. It is important for women (and men) to raise up such neglected texts for all to hear.

PRAYER SERVICE FOR THE SECOND WEEK OF EASTER

THEME: Resurrection!

GATHERING RITUAL: Come together, as for Easter week, in a brightly lighted and joyfully decorated space with a large white candle burning and with music playing. (Suggestion: Handel's "Hallelujah Chorus")

FOCUS TIME: Join in singing the "Hallelujah Chorus" or other "Alleluia" song.

Leader: Jesus is risen, Alleluia!
All: JESUS IS RISEN, ALLELUIA!
Leader: This is the day our God has made. Let us rejoice and
      be glad.
All: JESUS IS RISEN, ALLELUIA!
Reader: [A Reading from the Gospel of John]
      But Mary [of Magdala] stood weeping outside the tomb and, as she wept, she stooped to look into the tomb. And she saw two angels in white, sitting where the body of Jesus had lain, one at the head and one at the feet. They said to her, "Woman, why are you weeping?" She said to them, "Because they have taken away my Lord, and I do not know where they have laid him." Saying this, she turned round and saw Jesus standing, but she did not know that it was Jesus. Jesus said to her, "Woman, why are you weeping? Whom do you seek?" Supposing him to be the gardener, she said to him, "Sir, if you have carried him away, tell me where you have laid him and I will take him away." Jesus said to her, "Mary." She turned around and said to him, "Rabboni!" (which means Teacher). Jesus said to her, "Do not cling to me for I have not yet ascended to my Father, but go find the others and tell them, I am ascending to my Father, . . . to my God and your God." Mary went and said to the disciples, "I have seen the Lord!" and she told them that he had said these things to her (John 20:11-18).

[Pause for a few moments of silence.]
[The following may be delivered aloud or read silently.]

All the Gospels report that women were the first to discover the empty tomb of Jesus on Easter morning. In John's Gospel, it is Mary of Magdala alone who first comes to the tomb. Seeing that the stone has been rolled away, she runs to tell Peter and the Beloved Disciple who also run to the tomb. Finding it empty, the two men return to their homes, "For they did not yet understand the scripture that he had to rise from the dead" (John 20:9**).

Mary alone remains, weeping at the tomb. Her womanly expression of affection and concern, expressed in her presence and in her tears, is rewarded by Jesus who appears in the person of the gardener and enters into dialogue with her, "Woman, why are you weeping? Whom are you looking for" (John 20:15**)? As evidenced in other characters in the Gospel of John, the essential component in coming to faith is personal encounter with Jesus. Mary seeks Jesus in faith as did the male disciples of chapter one and, like them, through a special faith experience supported by dialogue and presence, she comes to see beyond the human witness . . . to the person of Jesus. "Sir, if you carried him away, tell me where you laid him . . ." (20:15**). And Jesus says to her, "Mary!" She turns and replies, "Rabbouni!" (which means Teacher). Calling her by name, Jesus leads his friend Mary to faith in him as her risen Lord.

Mary's response to Jesus when he calls her by name recalls the parable of the Good Shepherd, "the sheep hear his voice, or he calls his own sheep by name and leads them out. When he has driven out all his own, he walks ahead of them, and the sheep follow him, because they recognize his voice" (John 10:3,4**). Noted Johannine scholar Raymond Brown points to this connection as "another proof" that a woman could be an intimate disciple of Jesus. Brown makes the further connection that the terminology, "his own" (10:3-5) is the same expression used at the Last Supper, "He loved his own in the world and he loved them to the end" (13:1**). Brown concludes, "It is clear that John has no hesitation in placing a woman in the same category of relationship to Jesus as the Twelve . . ." (1979, p. 192).

Mary is included not only in the "primary Christian category for John" (CBD, p. 191), that of discipleship, she is also explicitly sent by Jesus to bear witness to his resurrection. After telling her not to try to cling to him, not to hold on to her earthly image of him, Jesus sends Mary to the disciples with a message, "'I am going to my Father . . . to my God and your God'" (20:17*). From now on, it will be through the Holy Spirit that the gift of intimate communion with Jesus for which Mary longs is possible in a new way. It is through the Spirit that Jesus continues his intimate, life-giving relationship with disciples.

It is through Mary of Magdala that the message of hope is first delivered to the Christian community. A woman is the first to proclaim what becomes the standard apostolic announcement of the resurrection, "I have seen the Lord" (20:18). This same announcement is used by Paul to substantiate his own claim of apostleship, "Am I not an apostle? Have I not seen the Lord" (cf. I Cor 9:1)? Sent by the risen Lord himself, Mary of Magdala is the "apostle to the apostles," the most prominent Johannine witness to the resurrection, a role traditionally associated with Peter who, in John's Gospel, sees at the tomb not the risen Lord, but only "the burial cloths there, and the cloth that had covered his head, . . ." (20:6,7*).

Once again, John's literary style and his particular tradition provide some unique insights into the quality of personal relationship with Jesus that leads to faith in him. The meeting of the risen Jesus with Mary of Magdala portrays his relationship with her, a woman, as one of special affection and respect. As in previous encounters with the Woman of Samaria and Martha and Mary of Bethany, Jesus affirms women disciples as persons and he enables them to see beyond their previous expectations. In calling her by name and manifesting himself to her as the Risen Lord, Jesus recognizes Mary's love and commitment to him, but he also challenges her to develop her real potential as a woman who sees with clarity into the true nature of things and whose faithfulness allows her to risk bearing testimony to that reality. Jesus liberates her in the very act of choosing her and sending her to engage in his mission.

[Pause here again for a moment of silent response.]

DISCUSSION/REFLECTION:

What special qualities allow Mary to hear the voice of the risen Christ in the words of the gardener?

What enables her to see the face of Christ in the person of the gardener?

Where might we hear the voice of Christ or see his face?

ACTION: Make a special effort this week to look for the face of Christ in ordinary people (like the gardener) and to hear the voice of Christ as he calls you by name. Tell other women (and interested men) about this moving and often neglected resurrection narrative.

CLOSING: [Cf. Psalm 23 & John 10:14-18]

Leader: We have seen the Lord!

All: WE HAVE SEEN THE LORD!

Leader: I am the good shepherd.

    I know my own and my own know me;

    You have nothing to fear.

    To meadows of green grass I lead you;

    In waters of repose I restore your soul.

All: WE HAVE SEEN THE LORD!

Leader: Though you pass through a dark valley, do not fear.

    My rod and my staff are there to hearten you.

    I prepare a table before you.

All: WE HAVE SEEN THE LORD!

Leader: I lay down my life for my sheep, but no one takes it

       from me; I have power to lay it down and power to

       take it up again. I am the good shepherd.

All: WE HAVE SEEN THE LORD!

Leader: I know my sheep and mine know me. Goodness and kindness surround you every day of your life. I anoint your head with oil; my cup brims over.

All: WE HAVE SEEN THE LORD!

CLOSING SONG: Repeat Handel's "Hallelujah Chorus" or another Easter song. Additional suggestion: "You Shall Be My Witnesses," by Miriam Therese Winter (WomanSong, 1987).

THE THIRD WEEK OF EASTER

In Cycle A, the Gospel for this Third Sunday of Easter is Luke 24:13-35, the story of two disciples traveling home from Jerusalem to Emmaus on the evening of that first day of the week. Cycle B continues with Luke 24:35-48 which opens with the same disciples recounting what they had seen on the road, and Cycle C continues the Gospel from John (21:1-19), appearances at the Sea of Tiberias. The readings from Acts in each cycle record one of Peter's discourses.

In the reflection that follows, we focus on the the reading from Cycle A, two disciples on the road to Emmaus. Traditionally, it has been assumed, wherever a reference to "disciples" appears that, unless it is specifically stated that they are women, the disciples are male. That has been true, not only of official teaching and preaching, but also of personal reflection on the part of women, as well as men. (That this is true for the personal reflection of women is borne out in informal surveys I have taken of groups of women, small in number, but representative samplings.) Such unimaginative and limiting mindsets have precluded women from putting themselves and their experiences in the reflection except in secondary and analogical ways.

Since recent biblical scholarship has begun to affirm that women were included as disciples of Jesus and that they were participating members of the early Christian community, including roles of leadership, many women are finding that the Scriptures come alive for them in new ways as they include themselves in such passages. In the reflection that follows, we know the name of one of the disciples, Cleopas. The unnamed disciple may be a man or a woman. The two could have been a married couple, likely if we assume that their destination, the place where they invite Jesus to spend the night and break bread with him, was their home. You are encouraged (women and men), at least this one time, to think of the unnamed disciple as female.

PRAYER SERVICE FOR THE THIRD WEEK OF EASTER

THEME: Resurrection

GATHERING RITUAL: Come together, as in previous weeks of the Easter Season, in a brightly lighted and joyfully decorated space with a large white candle burning and with music playing. [Suggestion: Handel's "Hallelujah Chorus."]

FOCUS TIME: Join in singing the "Hallelujah Chorus" or other appropriate song. [If available, "Were Not Our Hearts?" words and music by Carey Landry: North American Liturgy Resources,1973, would be especially appropriate.]

Leader: Jesus is risen, Alleluia!

All: JESUS IS RISEN, ALLELUIA!

Leader: "For where two or three are gathered together in my name, there am I in the midst of them" (Matthew 18:20*).

All: JESUS IS RISEN, ALLELUIA!

Leader: The cup of blessing that we bless, is it not a participation in the blood of Christ? The bread that we break, is it not a participation in the body of Christ? Because the loaf of bread is one, we, though many, are one body, for we all partake of the one loaf (I Corinthians 10:16*).

All: JESUS IS RISEN, ALLELUIA!

Leader: A reading from the Gospel of Luke

Narrator: On that first day of the week, two disciples of Jesus were making their way to a village named Emmaus seven miles distant from Jerusalem, discussing as they went all that had happened. In the course of their lively exchange, Jesus himself approached and began to walk with them. But their eyes were kept from recognizing him.

Jesus: What are you discussing with each other as you walk along?

Narrator: They halted in distress . . .

Cleopas: Are you the only person around who does not know the things that have happened?

Jesus: What things?

Cleopas: All those that had to do with Jesus of Nazareth, a prophet powerful in word and deed and in the eyes of God and all the people; how our chief priests and rulers delivered him up to be condemned to death, and crucified him. We were hoping that he was the one that would set Israel free.

(Mary): And this is not all: two whole days have gone by since it all happened and some women from our group have just brought us some astonishing news. They were at the tomb before dawn and when they did not find the body, they came back to tell us they had seen a vision of angels who declared he was alive. Then some other of our friends went to the tomb and found everything exactly as the women had reported, but Jesus they did not see.

Jesus: How foolish you are! How slow to believe the full message of the prophets! Was it not ordained that the Christ should suffer and so enter into his glory?

Narrator: Then, starting with Moses and going through all the prophets, he explained to them the passages throughout the scriptures that were about himself. And when they drew near to the village to which they were going, he acted as if he were going further, but they pressed him:

(Mary): Stay with us. It is nearly evening; the day is practically over.

Narrator: So he went in to stay with them. Now, while he was with them at table, he took the bread and said the blessing; then he broke it and handed it to them And their eyes were opened. And they recognized him, but he had vanished from their sight. Then they said to each other,

Cleopas & (Mary): Were not our hearts burning within us as he talked to us on the road and explained the scriptures to us?

Narrator: They set out that instant and returned to Jerusalem where they told the others their story of what had happened on the road and how they had come to recognize him in the breaking of bread (cf. Luke 24:13-35).

All: If available, sing "Are Not Our Hearts" (as above), or pause for a moment of silence.

[The following may be delivered aloud or read silently.]

The story we have just heard is one of the most beautiful and engaging passages in all of Scripture. It is a model for so many occasions and settings, for so many experiences. The story is about a journey, a literal journey from Jerusalem through the Judean countryside to the village of Emmaus and back again to Jerusalem. The journey is also symbolic: a movement from despair to hope, from sadness to joy, from unfaith to faith. It is the journey of discipleship: from death to life, from bad news to GOOD NEWS that is born out of experience and proclaimed with unwavering faith.

"Two of them," two disciples walk along. One is named Cleopas; the other is unnamed by the evangelist, perhaps so that the reader might identify with the nameless one and thus enter the story, becoming one of the dialogue partners. "Two of them," two friends—perhaps a man and a woman, possibly a married couple—walk along the road. And Jesus draws near and walks along with them. The one who has all the answers asks a question. "What are you talking about as you walk along?"

Only after he has listened to their distress, allowed them to tell their story does he begin to interpret for them the things concerning himself. Jesus does not force himself upon them; he walks with them at the same time he is leading them to a deeper understanding of themselves and of the things that have come to pass in their lives. Jesus simply offers his message and appears to be moving on.

Resurrection involves leave-taking; it involves letting go. But his letting go seems to have invited their response: "Stay with us." Cleopas and his companion (Mary) hunger for more. So, at the table, he fills their hunger with his own presence in the breaking of bread. But when their eyes are opened, he disappears from their sight. They are left, as we are, to reflect on his presence—in their own hearts, in the breaking of bread, and wherever two or three are gathered in his name. They are left, as we are, to retell the story of what had happened on the road and how they had recognized him in the breaking of bread. "Were not our hearts burning within us as he talked to us on the road?"

[Pause for a moment of silence.]

REFLECTION/DISCUSSION:

Whom, among the travelers I meet on the road of life, do I allow to influence me?

Whom do I allow to help me interpret the meaning of life?

Where, on the road, do I find the risen Christ?

ACTION: Take extra time this week to listen carefully to someone who has a story to tell (your spouse, your child, a friend, a stranger) and take special care to enter into his/her experience before offering advice or telling your own story.

CLOSING:
Leader: Jesus is risen, Alleluia!
All: JESUS IS RISEN, ALLELUIA!
Leader: Where two or three are gathered in my name, there
     am I in the midst of them (cf. Matthew 18:20).
All: JESUS IS RISEN, ALLELUIA!
Leader: The cup of blessing which we bless, is it not a partici-
     pation in the blood of Christ? The bread which we
     break, is it not a participation in the body of Christ?
     Because there is one bread, we who are many are one
     body for we all partake of the one bread (cf. I
     Corinthians 10:16).
All: JESUS IS RISEN, ALLELUIA!

[Participants share a loaf of bread and a cup of wine.]
[Conclude with "Were Not Our Hearts" (above) or another appropriate song.]

THE FOURTH WEEK OF EASTER

The theme of the Sunday Gospel for this Fourth Week of Easter in all three cycles is that of the Good Shepherd, a theme we anticipated in the Second Week as it relates to the narrative about the appearance of Jesus to Mary Magdalene, one of the sheep who belong to the Good Shepherd. Mary hears his voice when he calls her by name, and recognizes him. The readings from Acts in Cycles A and B for this Sunday focus on Peter's great Pentecost discourse, a summary of the Christian preaching about Jesus. In Cycle C we hear some of Paul's preaching in the synagogue at Antioch, patterned on Peter's discourses.

The reflection that follows is based on the first reading for Cycle B. Acts 4:8-12 reports Peter's response to the Sanhedrin, the rulers of Jerusalem, who are investigating his healing of a crippled man "in the name of Jesus Christ of Nazareth" (4:10). The reading for reflection that follows here describes that healing and the response to it, alongside a healing by Jesus from the Gospel of Luke. The two pericopes are parallel in content; they are also parallel in the contrasting responses of the people gathered and that of the authorities who question Peter in Acts, just as the ruler of the synagogue questions Jesus in the Gospel.

PRAYER SERVICE FOR THE FOURTH WEEK OF EASTER

THEME: Easter faith: Good news for the outcasts

GATHERING RITUAL: Come together, as in the previous weeks of Easter, in a brightly lighted and joyfully decorated space with a large white candle burning and with music playing. [Suggestion: Handel's "Hallelujah Chorus."]

FOCUS TIME: Join in singing the "Hallelujah Chorus" or other Easter song.

Leader: Let us listen to a set of parallel readings from the Book of Acts and the Gospel of Luke (cf. Acts 3:1-10; 4:12, 21 & Luke 13:10-17).

Reader 1: Now Peter and John were going up to the temple at the hour of prayer. And a man lame from birth was being carried to the gate of the temple to ask alms of those who entered.

Reader 2: Now Jesus was teaching in one of the synagogues on the Sabbath and there was a woman who had lived with a spirit of infirmity for eighteen years. She was bent over and could not fully straighten herself out.

Reader 1: Seeing Peter and John about to go into the temple, he asked for alms. And Peter directed his gaze at him. . . . and said, "I have no silver and gold, but I give you what I have; in the name of Jesus Christ of Nazareth, walk." And he took him by the hand and raised him up; and immediately his feet and ankles were made strong.

Reader 2: And when Jesus saw her he called her and said to her, "Woman, you are freed from your infirmity." And he laid his hands on her.

Reader 1: And leaping up he stood and walked and entered the temple, . . . walking and leaping and praising God.

Reader 2: And immediately she stood upright and began to praise God.

Reader 1: And as they were speaking the priests and captain of the temple and the Sadducees came upon them, annoyed . . . and they arrested them. . . . And on the morrow they inquired, "By what power or by what name did you do this?"

Reader 2: But the ruler of the synagogue, indignant because Jesus had healed on the Sabbath, said to the people, "There are six days on which to work; come on those days and be healed and not on the Sabbath."

Reader 1: Then Peter, filled with the Holy Spirit, said to them, "Be it known to you all...that by the name of Jesus Christ of Nazareth, whom you crucified, whom God raised from the dead, by him this man is standing before you well. This is the stone which was rejected by you the builders, but which has become the corner-stone. And there is salvation in no one else, for there is no other name under heaven by which we are saved."

Reader 2: Then Jesus answered, "You hypocrites! Does not each of you on the Sabbath untie your ox or your ass from the manger and lead it away to water it? And ought not this woman, a daughter of Abraham [and Sarah] be loosed from her bond on the Sabbath day?" As he said this, all his adversaries were put to shame.

Reader 1: And when they had further threatened them, they let them go, finding no way to punish them, because of the people; for all praised God for what had happened.

Reader 2: And all the people rejoiced at all the glorious things that were done by him.

[Pause for a moment of silent reflection.]
[The following may be delivered aloud or read silently.]

"And ought not this woman, a daughter of Abraham [and Sarah], be loosed from her bonds?"

Luke's "job description" for Jesus and for all who would be disciples is spelled out during the first visit of Jesus to the synagogue in chapter four of Luke's Gospel, the first of his two-volume work. Jesus came "to preach good news to the poor, to proclaim liberty to captives, to recover sight for the blind, and to set at liberty those who are oppressed" (Luke 4:18). During the remainder of his public ministry, Jesus continues to proclaim the reign of God, accompanied by miracles such as the healing of the bent-over woman. In the Book of Acts, the followers of Jesus continue this work in his name. In the face of opposition, Jesus and, in his name, the first disciples continue day in and day out, the attack on evil, facing it head on whenever and wherever they meet it, announcing in word and deed the will of God to replace suffering and brokenness and death with peace and wholeness and new life.

The story of the bent-over woman in Luke's Gospel (paralleled in Acts by the story of the crippled man at the door of the temple) is little known but powerful. The first thing that happens to the woman is that Jesus notices her. Unlike the crippled man in Acts and most of the Gospel characters who are healed by Jesus, she does nothing to attract attention. She is simply present in the synagogue where Jesus is preaching. And Jesus is moved with pity at the sight of this woman, badly stooped, incapable of standing erect. He sees the suffering, the pain, and he calls out to her, "Woman, you are freed from your infirmity." And he reaches out and touches her, a startling gesture in face of ritual rules about touching women and others considered unclean. And he lays his hands upon her. Jesus gives her the amazing news that she is free! And Luke says that she stood upright and praised God. And all the people rejoiced.

Jesus reaches out to this woman and makes her whole. And he identifies her with the title, "daughter of Abraham." The title is rare in Jewish literature and it appears nowhere else in the New Testament. Although we often hear of "sons (or children) of Abraham," this woman receives a special naming. Jesus includes her in the community of Israel. She is "daughter," part of the family; for the first time in the synagogue she is recognized as a human being (Nunnally-Cox, p.108).

But the very action that sets this bent-over woman free has bent out of shape the ruler of the synagogue. He addresses the crowd, but Jesus is the object of his indignation, "You have six days to come and be healed. . . ." The ruler of the synagogue, the religious leader, condemns the Son of God for breaking the Sabbath, but all the people gathered erupt in praise of God. The good news is proclaimed once again; people are more important than rules; another captive is set free; Jesus gives dignity to those rejected by society; another outcast, this woman, hidden in the pages of scripture, is free at last!

It was to people such as this, on the fringe of society, that Jesus paid special attention. It was due to such actions as this that Jesus disturbed the religious authorities who eventually put him to death. As John's Gospel points out, Jesus is the good shepherd who lays down his life for his sheep. They become his own; he calls them, women and men, by name and they recognize his voice and they follow him. In the name of Jesus, hidden possibilities are brought to light in people like Peter and Cleopas and Mary and the other members of the Jerusalem community, and, in the name of Jesus, hidden resources are given to people like ourselves. We too are expected to proclaim good news to the poor, to help the blind recover their sight, to set captives free, to cast out evil in the name of Jesus.

[Pause here for a moment of silence.]

REFLECTION/DISCUSSION: Reflect on the burdens that women have borne in our society and in our church. In what ways are women today continually "bent-over" by contemporary regulations or customs? Do you agree that contemporary disciples are called to cast out evil in the name of Jesus? How?

ACTION: Resolve to "stand upright" this week against a particular burden that is keeping you or someone else in a "bent-over" position.

CLOSING: [cf. Psalm 146]
Leader: She stood upright and gave praise to God.
All: SHE STOOD UPRIGHT AND GAVE PRAISE TO GOD.
Leader: Praise God, my soul! I mean to praise God all my life,
　　　Sing to my God as long as I live.
All: SHE STOOD UPRIGHT AND GAVE PRAISE TO GOD.
LEADER: Do not put trust in earthly power, or in mortals who
　　　cannot save.
　　　Happy we who have our God to help us, whose hope
　　　is fixed on God.
　　　Forever faithful, our God gives justice to those
　　　denied it,
　　　Food to the hungry and liberty to prisoners.
All: SHE STOOD UPRIGHT AND GAVE PRAISE TO GOD.
LEADER: Our God restores sight to the blind and straightens
　　　the bent.
　　　God protects the stranger and keeps the orphan and
　　　widow.
　　　Yahweh, our God, reigns forever and ever.
　　　Alleluia!
All: SHE STOOD UPRIGHT AND GAVE PRAISE TO GOD.

[Sing together a song that celebrates hidden resources called to life and action. Suggestions: "Sing of a Blessing," by Miriam Therese Winter, or "Myself Growing Older," by Marsie Silvestro.]

FIFTH WEEK OF EASTER

The Gospel readings for the Fifth Sunday of Easter are taken from the farewell discourse to the disciples at the Last Supper as presented in the Johannine account. Jesus will soon be leaving them, but they should not be troubled since he will send the Paraclete who will teach them everything and in whose power they will do the works that Jesus does, and greater works than these (John 14:12). The first readings, from Acts, speak of some of the hardships the earliest community faces in attempting to proclaim the Gospel in word and deed. In Cycles B and C we read of persecution and trials suffered by Paul. In Cycle A we get a glimpse of some of the internal problems faced by these early Christians and the democratic way in which the community attempts to resolve them.

The reflection that follows focuses on the response of the earliest Jerusalem community to the expressed need for a diversity of ministries and on the expansion of ministry in the communities founded by Paul. These communities seem to have taken for granted that women, as well as men, are called to participate in the ministry of Christ's Church just as women, as well as men, were included among the disciples of Jesus as recorded in all four Gospels.

PRAYER SERVICE FOR THE FIFTH WEEK OF EASTER

THEME: Resurrection—the good news is proclaimed!

GATHERING RITUAL: Come together, as in the previous weeks of Easter, in a brightly lighted and joyfully decorated space with a large white candle burning and with music playing. (Suggestion: Handel's "Hallelujah Chorus.")

FOCUS TIME: Join in singing the "Hallelujah Chorus" or other Easter song.

Leader: Jesus is risen, Alleluia!
All: JESUS IS RISEN, ALLELUIA!
Leader: The good news is proclaimed and the dead are
       raised to life.

All: JESUS IS RISEN, ALLELUIA!

Leader: The good news continues to spread and the number
      of believers increases.

All: JESUS IS RISEN, ALLELUIA!

GOSPEL READING: [from the Book of Acts]

> In those days, as the number of disciples grew, the ones
> who spoke Greek complained that their widows were
> being neglected in the daily distribution of food, as com-
> pared with the widows of those who spoke Hebrew. The
> Twelve assembled the community of the disciples and
> said, "It is not right for us to neglect the word of God in
> order to wait on the tables. Look around among your own
> number for seven [who are] acknowledged to be deeply
> spiritual and prudent, and we shall appoint them to this
> task. This will permit us to concentrate on prayer and the
> ministry of the word." The proposal was unanimously
> accepted by the community. Following this, they selected
> Stephen, a disciple filled with faith and the Holy Spirit;
> Philip, Prochorus, Nicanor, Timon, Parmenas and
> Nicolaus of Antioch who had been a convert to Judaism.
> They presented these to the apostles who first prayed over
> them and then imposed hands on them. The word of God
> continued to spread, while at the same time the number of
> disciples in Jerusalem enormously increased (cf. Acts 6:1-7).

[Pause for a moment of silent reflection.]
[The following may be delivered aloud or read silently.]

Look around among your own number for seven who are
acknowledged to be deeply spiritual and prudent, and we
shall appoint them. . . . They presented these to the apostles
who first prayed over them and then imposed hands on
them. The word of God continued to spread, while at the
same time the number of disciples . . . enormously increased.

As the number of disciples increases, it becomes necessary
to appoint additional ministers. In this passage, although the
authority of the Twelve is highlighted as they respond to the

community's complaint and as they lay hands on the new ministers, a democratic style of governing is also evident since the community shares in the selection process. "Look around among your own number. . . ." While it is not completely clear what the problem is, it has something to do with members not being well-served. And, while it is stated that the "seven" are charged with waiting on table, nowhere in Acts is there any record of their fulfilling this role (unless it has more to do with the sacramental "breaking of bread" than is evident in the text.) Rather, those about whom we hear more later, Stephen and Philip, do what is described as the role of the Twelve ministry of the word and prayer (6:4).(For example, in Acts 7, Stephen preaches, and in Chapter 8 Philip baptizes, preaches, and performs "signs" in the name of Jesus.) Luke may be incorporating a tradition here concerning the Seven who were "spirit-filled, independent Hellenistic missionaries" in order to present them (and all missionaries) as subservient to the Twelve (Karris, *Invitation to Acts*, p.76).

It seems appropriate to raise here also the topic of women disciples and ministers in the early church. While Luke devotes more time to women in his Gospel than in Acts, women are mentioned in this second volume of Luke-Acts both as disciples and as ministers. At the beginning of Acts, we find "several women, including Mary the mother of Jesus," who join the male disciples "in continuous prayer" in the upper room (1:14) and in Peter's speech in chapter two, we learn about the fulfillment of prophecy as he quotes the book of Joel, "sons and daughters prophesy . . ." and the Spirit is "poured out on men and women" (cf. 2:17,18). In chapter eight we read of both women and men being persecuted by Saul (8:3).

During Paul's second missionary journey, we learn that the mother of Timothy has become a believer (16:1), and at Thesalonika a number of wealthy women from the Jewish synagogue are convinced by Paul's preaching and join him and Silas (17:4) as did many Greek women from the upper classes (17:12). After Paul's speech in Athens before the council of the Areopagus, a woman called Damaris, along with

Dionysius the Areopagite and others attached themselves to him and became believers (17:34).

While most of the above references to women are omitted from the lectionary readings, we do find on Saturday of the third week of Easter an account (9:32-42) of the healing by Peter of both a paralyzed man from Lydda named Aeneas and a woman disciple from nearby Joppa named Tabitha (in Aramaic) or Dorcas (in Greek). Called a "disciple" by Luke, she "never tired of doing good or giving in charity" (cf. 9:36). When she suddenly becomes sick and dies, her friends send an urgent message to Peter to come and visit as soon as possible. That "Peter went back with them straight away" would seem to indicate his own respect for her. In an upper room in Joppa where the friends of Dorcas had been gathered in prayer and in tears, Peter kneels down alone and prays. Then he says to her, "Dorcas, stand up." And she opens her eyes and stands up. When the dead woman is presented alive to the community as a result of Peter's prayer, the miracle becomes known throughout all Joppa and many come to believe. Dorcas is the only character in the New Testament to be raised from the dead by a disciple of Jesus.

In addition to these women mentioned as believers, other women named in Acts are clearly ministers to the community—Mary, the mother of John was leader of a house church: "Peter went to the house of Mary . . . where many were gathered together and were praying" (12:12); as was Lydia, whose house seems to have become a center of missionary activity (16:15, 40). In Acts 21 we read about the four daughters of Philip who prophesied (21:8,9).

From other sources we learn more about some of these female ministers mentioned in Acts. In Chapter 18, for example, Paul visits a married couple at Corinth, Priscilla (or Prisca) and Aquila who, like Paul himself, were tent-makers. Paul lodges with them while in Corinth and they work together as tent-makers during the week, while on the Sabbath they engage in debate in the synagogue (18:1-4). They become traveling companions with Paul and co-workers with him in ministry (18:18). We will meet Lydia and Priscilla again in the daily readings for the Sixth Week of Easter. For now, suffice it to say that women are participating members of the early communities both as disciples and as ministers (co-workers), gifted and chosen along with Peter, Paul and the others to proclaim the good news and to continue the healing ministry of Jesus "until he comes again."

[Pause for a few moments of silence.]

DISCUSSION/REFLECTION: The season of Easter is a time when the Church asks us to reflect together on the meaning of the Easter event for the life of our contemporary community of faith. We hear the Easter story told over and over in the Gospel readings and, in the first reading each Sunday from the book of Acts, we become familiar with the struggles and successes of the first community of Christians as they attempt to live as people of faith in the post-resurrection era. What do we learn from these reflections? What role models do we find?

ACTION: Make it a point this week to affirm the goodness in at least one woman you meet and, where appropriate, thank her for her contributions to family, church, or society.

CLOSING:

Leader: Jesus is risen, Allelluia!
All: JESUS IS RISEN, ALLELUIA!
Leader: The good news is proclaimed and the dead are raised to life.
All: JESUS IS RISEN, ALLELUIA!
Leader: The good news continues to spread and the number of believers increases.
All: JESUS IS RISEN, ALLELUIA!

[Join in singing a favorite Easter song, such as "Jesus Christ is Risen Today."]

SIXTH WEEK OF EASTER

The Gospels in all three cycles for the Sixth Sunday of Easter continue John's presentation of the discourse of Jesus at the Last Supper. They focus on love, the bond of love that exists between Jesus and his Father, the love of Jesus for the disciples and the necessity of love of disciples for Jesus and for one another. The selections from Acts focus on the Gentile mission. In Cycle A (Acts 8:5-8,14-17) the Samaritans receive Philip the deacon and his proclamation of the Gospel; Cycle B (Acts 10:25,26, 34,35,44-48) includes the encounter between Peter and Cornelius, and Cycle C (15:1-2,15-29) presents the decision of the great Jerusalem assembly that Gentiles would not be required to observe Jewish law in order to become Christian.

The selections chosen for the following reflection are taken from three of the daily liturgies for this Sixth Week of Easter, Monday, Thursday, and Saturday. They carry themes similar to those assigned to the Sundays of the three cycles; they are included here because they focus on the ministry of women and, perhaps for that very reason, are excluded from the Sunday lectionary. We meet Lydia and Prisca and we note a number of other women ministers to whom Paul sends greetings in his letter to the Church at Rome. These include Phoebe the deacon and Junia, a female described by Paul as being "of note among the apostles" (cf. Romans 16:7).

PRAYER SERVICE FOR THE SIXTH WEEK OF EASTER

THEME:
Resurrection—the good news is proclaimed!

GATHERING RITUAL: Come together, as in the previous weeks of Easter, in a brightly lighted and joyfully decorated space with a large white candle burning and with music playing. [Suggestion: Handel's "Hallelujah Chorus."]

FOCUS TIME: Join in singing the "Hallelujah Chorus" or other Easter song.
Leader: Jesus is risen, Allelluia!

All: JESUS IS RISEN, ALLELUIA!

Leader: The good news is proclaimed and the Spirit of Jesus enlivens the Church.

All: JESUS IS RISEN, ALLELUIA!

Leader: The whole group of believers was united heart and soul.

All: JESUS IS RISEN, ALLELUIA!

GOSPEL READING [A collage of readings from Acts]:

Reader 1: Setting sail, therefore, from Troas, we made a direct voyage to Samothrace, and the following day to Neapolis, and from there to Philippi, a Roman colony and the leading city of that particular district of Macedonia. We remained in this city some days and on the Sabbath day we went outside the gate to the riverside where we supposed there was a place of prayer; and we sat down and spoke to the women who had come together. One who heard us was a devout woman named Lydia, from the city of Thyatira, who was in the purple dye trade. She listened to us and the Lord opened her heart to hear what Paul was saying. After she and her household had been baptized she sent us an invitation: "If you really think me a true believer in the Lord, come to my house and stay with us," and she would take no refusal (cf. Acts 16:13; Monday, Sixth Week of Easter).

From the prison [Paul and Silas] went to Lydia's house where all the brethren were gathered and gave them some encouragement . . . (cf. Acts 16:40).

Reader 2: After this Paul left Athens and went to Corinth where he met a Jew called Aquila whose family came from Pontus. He and his wife Priscilla had recently left Italy. . . . Paul went to visit them and, when he found they were tent-makers, of the same trade as himself, he lodged with them and they worked together (cf. Acts 18:1-3; Thursday, Sixth Week of Easter).

120

Reader 3: An Alexandrian Jew named Apollos now arrived in Ephesus. He was an eloquent man, with a sound knowledge of the Scriptures, and yet, though he had been given instruction in the Way of the Lord and preached with great spiritual earnestness and was accurate in all the details he taught about Jesus, he had only experienced the baptism of John. When Priscilla and Aquila heard him speak boldly in the synagogue, they took an interest in him and gave him further instructions about the Way (cf. Acts 18:24-26; Saturday, Sixth Week of Easter).

[Pause for a few moments of silence.]
[The following may be delivered aloud or read silently.]

While we find little about the ministry of women in the lectionary readings for Sundays, we find these three passages in the daily readings for the Sixth Week of Easter. Lydia, a wealthy and competent business woman meets Paul on his first visit to Philippi. She and her household are baptized. Now, it is helpful for us to understand the significance of the term "household."

In New Testament times the household was regarded as a basic political unit. In addition to members of the immediate family, slaves, freedmen, servants, laborers, and sometimes business associates and tenants were included. The closeness of the household unit offered the security and sense of belonging not provided by larger political and social structures (Malherbe, *Social Aspects of Early Christianity*, p. 69).

Lydia may well be the first European convert to Christianity and, on her own initiative, Lydia's household becomes the base for the first Christian mission in Europe, a house church where the community gathers for comfort and support. In these days of house-churches, the head of the household was the usual person to preside over the "breaking of bread" in the absence of one of the apostles or other appointed leaders. It seems likely that Lydia and other women heads of households functioned as presiders at

Eucharist before the emergence of official church office (Nunnaly-Cox, p. 128). Lydia may well serve as a role model for the many business women of today who juggle the responsibilities of home and office and who also find time to volunteer their talents in service to their religious and civic communities.

Prisca and her husband Aquila exercise a team ministry, are co-workers with Paul, and lead Christian communities that meet in their house. Prisca is established as a church leader, a missionary apostle, and catechist. The couple is mentioned six times in the New Testament and four of those times her name is listed before that of her husband, highly unusual and probably indicating that she was the leader of this "couple ministry." It is at least indicative of the strong role she played in the ministry of the early Church.

Texts like this help us to appreciate the attitude of Saint Paul toward women and toward the teamwork of married people in the apostolate of the Church. This couple not only acted as a welcoming committee at Ephesus but also as educators in theology. To dialogue with someone as sharp and knowledgeable as Apollos and to lead him . . . meant that the couple were well-informed, capable of . . . advancing the discussion, and most of all, open to incisive insights from the Holy Spirit (Stuhlmueller, *Biblical Meditations for the Easter Season*, p. 121).

In Romans 16 (see below) we read that Paul is grateful to Prisca and Aquila for risking their lives on his behalf, an indication of their influential status. And there is no suggestion of subordination in Prisca's relationship to her husband or to Paul. Equality of women and men in ministry in these Pauline communities seems to be taken for granted.

Some references to the ministry of women in the Pauline corpus include the following (emphasis mine):

I commend to you our sister Phoebe, deacon of the Church at Cenchrae, that you may receive her in the Lord as befits the saints, and help her in whatever way she may require from you, for she has been a helper of many and of myself as well. Greet Prisca and Aquila, my fellow workers in Christ Jesus who risked their necks for my life, to whom not only I, but all the Churches of the Gentiles give thanks; greet also the church in their house. . . . Greet Mary, who has worked hard among you. Greet Andronicus and Junias, . . . of note among the apostles. . . . Greet those workers in the Lord, Tryphaena and Tryphosa. Greet the beloved Persis who has worked hard in the Lord. Greet . . . Nereus and his sister, and Olympas and all the saints who are with them (cf. Romans 16: 1-16).

The churches of Asia send greetings. Aquila and Prisca, together with the church in their house, send you hearty greetings in the Lord (cf. I Corinthians 16:19).

It has been reported to me by Chloe's people that there has been quarreling among you (cf. I Corinthians 1:11).

Please give my greetings to the friends at Laodicea and to Nympha and the church which meets at her house (cf. Colossians 4:15).

These and other New Testament passages, as well as extra-biblical sources, give us some limited information and provide material for further "hints and guesses" concerning the role of women in these New Testament communities. They also give us "hints and guesses" about possibilities for the diversification of ministry in our own time when there seems to be a shortage of vocations to the ordained priesthood, particularly in the Roman Catholic Church. It also gives us pause to think about the abundance of gifts and talents that remain untapped in our contemporary Christian communities. Let us continue to pray as we wait for the day when, once again, the gifts of the Spirit will be recognized, called forth, and validated, wherever they are found.

[Pause for a few moments of silence.]

DISCUSSION/REFLECTION: Paul uses the same title, "diakonos" for Phoebe in Romans 16 as he does elsewhere for Timothy and others. When used of men, it is traditionally translated "deacon" or "minister." When used for Phoebe, the term has been translated "helper" or "deaconess." What do you think accounts for this difference in translation? Feminist scripture scholars insist that we look critically at such texts from the perspective of women. What might we learn about women in ministry from such texts?

ACTION: Take some time this week to familiarize yourself with these and other New Testament passages concerning women. Share your learnings with at least one other person (a friend, your spouse, your children, your pastor).

CLOSING:

Leader: Jesus is risen, Allelluia!

All: JESUS IS RISEN, ALLELUIA!

Leader:The good news spreads and the Spirit of Jesus
	enlivens the Church.

All: JESUS IS RISEN, ALLELUIA!

Leader: The whole group of believers are united heart and
	soul.

All: JESUS IS RISEN, ALLELUIA!

Leader: Women and men testify with great power to the res-
	urrection of Jesus.

All: JESUS IS RISEN, ALLELUIA!

[Sing together an appropriate song. Suggestions: "Hear God's Word" or "A New Day Dawns," by Miriam Therese Winter, WomanSong, 1987.]

SEVENTH WEEK OF EASTER

The Gospel readings for all three Cycles on the Sunday between the feasts of Ascension and Pentecost are from John's accounts of the final prayer of Jesus on the night before he died. In Cycle A (John 17:1-11), Jesus speaks of the completion of the work which he has been given. The "hour" has come for him to leave this world and he begins the prayer for his disciples which continues in Cycles B (17:12-19). In C (17:20-26), Jesus prays for future believers, "all who will believe in him through their word."

The reading from Acts for Cycle A is a summary statement, the conclusion of the prologue to Acts, showing the disciples in the "upper room," immediately after returning to Jerusalem from Mount Olivet after the Ascension. They continue in prayer while they await the fulfillment of the promise of Jesus to send the Paraclete. In Cycle B, chapter one of Acts continues as the disciples, still gathered in the upper room, select Matthias to replace Judas, reconstituting the "twelve." In Cycle C, the passage concerning the death of Stephen, the first Christian martyr, is read, a reminder that followers of Jesus can expect suffering as well as joy, peace, and the other fruits of the Spirit.

In the reflection that follows, the focus is on the reading from Acts for Cycle A (1:12-14), the gathering of disciples in the upper room, including Mary, the mother of Jesus, who is presented in the Gospels as a model of discipleship.

PRAYER SERVICE FOR THE SEVENTH WEEK OF EASTER

THEME: Discipleship

GATHERING RITUAL: Come together in a quiet space with a large white candle burning and soft instrumental music playing.

FOCUS TIME: Join in singing "Come, Holy Spirit."

Leader: Jesus is risen, Allelluia!

All: JESUS IS RISEN, ALLELUIA!

Leader: After his passion, he had shown himself alive to them in many demonstrations.

All: JESUS IS RISEN, ALLELUIA!

Leader: The whole group of believers was united heart and soul.

All: JESUS IS RISEN, ALLELUIA!

Leader: This Jesus who was taken up from you into heaven will come in the same way as you saw him go.

All: JESUS IS RISEN, ALLELUIA!

Leader: A Reading from the Gospel of John and the Book of Acts.

Reader 1: Jesus lifted up his eyes to heaven and said, "Father, the hour has come; glorify your son, that the son may glorify you, since you have given him power over all flesh, to give eternal life to all whom you have given him. . . . I have given you glory on earth by finishing the work you have given me to do. . . . I have made your name known to those you gave me . . . and they have kept your word . . . and know in truth that I came from you; and they have believed that you sent me. . . . I pray for them, for those you have given me, for they are yours; all mine are yours and yours are mine, and I am glorified in them. And now I am no more in the world, but they are in the world and I am coming to you (cf. John 17:1-11; Cycle A).

[Pause here for a moment of silent reflection.]

Reader 2: [After Jesus was taken up into heaven], they returned to Jerusalem, . . . to the upper room where they were staying, Peter and John and James and Andrew [and the other]. Together they devoted themselves to constant prayer. There were some women in their company and Mary, the mother of Jesus, and his brothers (cf. Acts 1:12-14; Cycle A).

[Pause again for a few moments of silence.]
[The following may be delivered aloud or read silently.]

"There were some women in their company and Mary, the mother of Jesus."

During this week, between Ascension and Pentecost, we observe the early disciples, through the eyes of Luke, waiting in an upper room for the outpouring of the promised Spirit who is to guide them and empower them in the absence of Jesus. Among the disciples is Mary, the mother of Jesus. It is significant that Luke names her here as a member of the believing community, waiting with the others in prayer; it gives us a hint of how the first Christians viewed her position in their midst. Earlier, in the Gospel of Luke, Jesus had praised his mother as a model disciple, one who "hears the word of God and keeps it" (Luke 8:19;11:28).

While Luke describes a time span of forty days between the resurrection and the ascension, followed by a period of waiting before the coming of the Spirit, John's Gospel speaks of the death/resurrection/ascension/sending of the Spirit as if it is one act. He refers to this single event as the "hour." In the selection from the Gospel of John for this final Sunday of Easter, we hear the words of the final prayer of Jesus for his disciples, uttered on the night before he died, "Father, the hour has come."

The "hour" is first mentioned in the Gospel of John at the marriage feast at Cana, the beginning of the public ministry, when Jesus performs the first "sign" through which he manifests his glory and disciples come to believe in him. Here, Jesus replies to his mother's request for a miracle, "Woman [a title of respect] what have you to do with me?" (Or "What is the nature of our relationship?") "My hour has not yet come." (Or possibly a question, "Has my hour come?" [McPolin, p.24]). The only other time the mother of Jesus appears in the Gospel of John is at the cross when his hour has finally come. Again, Jesus calls her "Woman."

Seeing his mother and the disciple he loved standing near her, he said to his mother, "Woman, this is your son!" Then he said to the disciple, "This is your mother!" And from that hour the disciple made a place for her in his home (cf. John 19:26.27).

The author of John's Gospel, like Luke and the other evangelists, presents the essential relationship of Mary to her Son as that of discipleship. Mary is the primary believer, the model disciple. Together with the other women, she follows him along the way and stands by the cross in a relationship of faith. In the upper room, she waits and prays, along with the others, for empowerment through the Spirit of her Son. The gift of the Spirit is the fruit of prayer; it requires on our part a spirit of openness to hearing and keeping the word of God. As it was sought in prayer by those first members of the Christian community, so it must be sought anew in our time by constant prayer. Come, Holy Spirit, Come!

[Pause here for another moment of silence.]

DISCUSSION/REFLECTION: Mary, the mother of Jesus, is presented to us in the Gospels and Acts as a disciple, one who "hears the Word of God and lives it out." We know little else about her from the New Testament. How has our past tradition presented Mary? Can Mary be appropriated by contemporary women and men as a role model? What can we learn from her?

ACTION: Aware of our own needs and those of our world, let us pray this week for openness in our hearts and minds and in the hearts and minds of the leaders of our Church to the movement of the Spirit in our time. Let us cooperate with those who work for justice so that all of us can enjoy the peace that is the fruit of justice and the gift of the Spirit.

CLOSING:
Leader: Jesus is risen, Alleluia!
All: JESUS IS RISEN, ALLELUIA!
Leader: After his passion, he had shown himself alive to
        them in many demonstrations.
All: JESUS IS RISEN, ALLELUIA!
Leader: The whole group of believers was united heart and
        soul.
All: JESUS IS RISEN, ALLELUIA!
Leader: This Jesus who was taken up from you into heaven
        will come in the same way as you saw him go.
All: JESUS IS RISEN, ALLELUIA!

[All sing "Come, Holy Spirit" or another appropriate song. Suggestion: "We Are the World," by Miriam Therese Winter, WOMANSONG.]

THE FEAST OF PENTECOST

The liturgical readings for Pentecost Sunday are the same for all three cycles. The Gospel (John 20:19-23) is a portion of that used on the Second Sunday of Easter.

On the evening of the first day of the week, the doors being shut, Jesus came and stood among them and said, "Peace with you. . . . Receive the Holy Spirit."

While John's Gospel situates the return of Jesus to his Father and the coming of the Holy Spirit on the same day as the resurrection, Luke-Acts describes the Ascension on the fortieth day after Easter and situates the coming of the Spirit on the fiftieth day, the Jewish feast of Pentecost. The first liturgical reading for the feast is that of Acts 2:1-11, Luke's dramatic description of the descent of the Spirit and its immediate effect on the disciples who are found gathered in one place. It appears to be in the same room described in Chapter one, the upper room where Mary and the "brothers" of Jesus were gathered with the "eleven" and the other women. The second reading is from Paul's First Letter to the Corinthians (12:3-7,12,13), a teaching on spiritual gifts. The reflection that follows will focus on the first and second readings, the coming of the Spirit and the use of gifts.

PRAYER SERVICE FOR THE FEAST OF PENTECOST

THEME: The spirit comes!

GATHERING RITUAL: Gather together around a large lighted candle with soft music playing in the background. [Suggestion: "Breath of God," by Miriam Therese Winters, WOMANSONG.]

FOCUS TIME: Join in singing the above or "Come, Holy Spirit."

Reader 1: [A reading from the book of Acts.]
And when they reached the city, they went to the upper room where they were staying, Peter and John and James and Andrew, and (the others). . . . With one accord they devoted themselves to prayer, together with the women

129

and Mary, the mother of Jesus, and with his brothers
(cf. Acts 1: 13, 14).

Leader: Jesus is risen, Alleluia!

All: JESUS IS RISEN, ALLELUIA!

Leader: I will send the Spirit to renew the face of the earth.

All: JESUS IS RISEN, ALLELUIA!

Leader: This is the day our God has made. Let us rejoice and
be glad.

All: JESUS IS RISEN, ALLELUIA!

Reader 2: [A reading from the book of Acts.]

When the day of Pentecost came they were all together in
one room. And suddenly a sound came from heaven like
the rush of a mighty wind, and it filled the entire house
where they were gathered. And there appeared to them
tongues of fire, distributed and resting on each one of them.
And they were all filled with the Holy Spirit. They began to
express themselves in foreign tongues and make bold
proclamation as the Spirit prompted them (cf. Acts 2:1-4).

Now there were dwelling in Jerusalem Jews from every
nation under heaven. . . . And they were bewildered
because they all heard them speaking in their own language. "Are not all those who are speaking Galileans?" . . .
And all were amazed and perplexed, saying, "What does
this mean?" Others, mocking, said, "They have been drinking too much new wine" (cf. Acts 2:5-13).

[Pause for silent reflection.]

Reader 3: [A reading from the first letter of Paul to the
Corinthians.]

No one can say, "Jesus is Lord," except by the Holy Spirit.
Now there are different gifts, but the same Spirit; there are
different ministries but the same Lord; there are different
works but the same God who accomplishes all of them in
everyone. To each person the manifestation of the Spirit is
given for the common good.

The body is one and has many members, but all the
members, many though they are, are one body. It was
in one Spirit that all of us, whether Jew or Greek, slave
or free, were baptized into one body.

All of us have been given to drink of the one Spirit (cf.
I Corinthians 12:3-7; 12-13).

[Pause again for silent reflection.]
[The following may be delivered aloud or read silently.]

Today we reflect upon the nature and origin of the
Church. The Christian Pentecost inaugurates a new moment
in the history of salvation. It is the birthday of the Church.
The "sound like the rush of a mighty wind" echoes the
Genesis account of the creation of the world when the wind
(usually translated *spirit*) hovered over the waters, and of the
creation of the first human person when the wind that is the
breath of life was breathed by God into the nostrils of the first
human person (LaVerdiere, *The Year of Luke*, p. 84).

> The wind is God's Spirit, effecting a new creation and
> filling the Church with God's creative life force. The
> tongues, like fire, represent God's purifying, sanctify-
> ing presence, consecrating the Church as prophetic
> speaker of God's word. . . . In spite of cultural and lin-
> guistic differences, everyone understands the . . . mes-
> sage about God's marvelous deeds. It reverses . . .
> Babel where human beings had ceased to understand
> each other (LaVerdiere, as above).

Similar to Luke's infancy narrative concerning the birth of
Jesus, this account of the birth of the Church evokes curiosity
and amazement on the part of some and rejection and mock-
ery on the part of others. "They have been drinking too much
wine." For the disciples in the upper room, however, this
experience is the fulfillment of the promise of Jesus to send
the Paraclete, the Helper, who would be with them always
and who would teach them all truth. For us, this annual celebration serves as a reminder that we too are gifted with the
creative Spirit of God, called to proclaim the good news and
to live it out in our particular moment in history.

Paul's letter to the community at Corinth is an instruction
concerning the use of these gifts of the Spirit. The letter is a
response to reports that there have been divisions among

them. Paul wants to make it clear that prophetic speaking comes only from those who have received the Spirit of God and who live in that same Spirit. The same spirit who gives the gift of faith, the recognition that Jesus is Lord, distributes all the other gifts and orchestrates them into a wonderful unity. Paul emphasizes the diversity and complementarity of gifts for the building up of the community.

But in a human community, especially where faith is weak, individual gifts can become divisive. They sometimes result in pride, arrogance, or envy. At times those called to serve in particular ways or in more public settings use their gifts in exclusive or self-aggrandizing ways, for their own advancement rather than for the good of the community. The Corinthian correspondence makes it clear that the early Church was not immune from such discord within. Perhaps that is why John's account of the sending of the Spirit, the Gospel chosen for this feast of Pentecost, includes a message about peace and forgiveness. "Peace be with you," Jesus says to them, "as the Father has sent me, so I send you." And he breathed on them and said, "Receive the Holy Spirit. If you forgive the sins of any, they are forgiven. . . ."

Clearly, the gifts of the Spirit do not remove problems or take away the human condition. In a community where the gifts of the Spirit abound, there is need also for forgiveness, the ability to see the Spirit of Jesus at work in each member, to affirm the differences among us as contributions to the common good, to work together for justice in relationships and toward a spirit of love and peace which is the fruit of justice. Paul mentions tensions evident in the early church, those between Jew and Greek and between slave and free. In our time he would undoubtedly mention tensions that continue to exist in our world between black and white, rich and poor, women and men, developed and developing countries.

> There are different kinds of spiritual gifts but the same
> Spirit; there are different forms of service but the same
> Lord; there are different workings but the same God
> who produces all of them in everyone. . . . and we
> were all given to drink of one Spirit (I Cor 12:4-6, 13*).

[Pause here for a moment of silence.]

<u>*DISCUSSION/REFLECTION:*</u> Pentecost is a time to celebrate our individual gifts and the diversity of ministries among us.

How do we use our gifts for the common good?

How do we call forth the gifts of one another?

<u>*CLOSING:*</u>

Leader: Jesus is risen, Alleluia!

All: JESUS IS RISEN, ALLELUIA!

Leader: Come, Holy Spirit, renew the face of the earth.

All: JESUS IS RISEN, ALLELUIA!

Leader: This is the day our God has made. Let us rejoice and be glad.

All: JESUS IS RISEN, ALLELUIA!

[Join together in spirit-filled song and dance followed by refreshments. Suggested songs are Handel's "Hallelujah Chorus" and/or some of the following selections from WomanSong, 1987 (above): "Come, Spirit," "You Shall Be My Witnesses," "We Are the Church," "Sing of a Blessing," "Circle Song." Additional suggestions: "From Generation to Generation" or "Claim Your Power" by Marsie Silvestro, Moonsong Productions, 1987.]

The biblical passages cited below are quoted directly from particular editions of biblical translations, which are hereby acknowledged. Complete publication information is given at the end of the bibliography which follows.

Page	Text	Source
3	Isaiah 63:17	New American Bible
4	Mark 3:35	Revised Standard Version
12	Luke 3:4	New American Bible
	2 Peter 3:10	New American Bible
16	Philippians 1:9-11	New American Bible
17	Isaiah 35:5	New American Bible
	Isaiah 61:1	New American Bible
	Zephaniah 3:15	New American Bible
30	Isaiah 9:1	New American Bible
	Isaiah 9:2,3	New American Bible
	Isaiah 9:5,6	New American Bible
43	Matthew 2:23	New American Bible
48	Mark 1:12,13	Revised Standard Version
84	Mark 14:9	Revised Standard Version
95	Acts 10:37-43	New American Bible
100	John 20:9,15	Revised Standard Version
	John 10:3,4	Revised Standard Version
101	John 13:1	Revised Standard Version
	John 20:17	Revised Standard Version
	John 20:6,7	Revised Standard Version
105	Matthew 18:20	Revised Standard Version
	I Cor, 10:16	Revised Standard Version
132	I Cor. 12:4-6,13	Revised Standard Version

Entries are divided into categories according to their usefulness as resources for background information and for plan planning prayer services. Some will overlap. Works cited are marked with an asterisk.

SCRIPTURAL & EARLY CHURCH BACKGROUND

* Brown, Raymond. *An Adult Christ at Christmas*. Collegeville, Minnesota: The Liturgical Press, 1978.

*_____. *The Community of the Beloved Disciple*. New York: Paulist Press, 1979.

*_____. *The Gospel According to John I-XII* (The Anchor Bible). New York: Doubleday,1966.

Collins, John J. "Isaiah" (*Collegeville Bible Commentary*, Dianne Bergant, gen. ed.). Collegeville, Minnesota: The Liturgical Press, 1986.

Deen, Edit. *All Of The Women Of The Bible*. San Francisco: Harper & Row Publications, 1988.

Dornisch, Loretta. *A Woman Reads the Gospel of Luke*. Collegeville, Minnesota: The Liturgical Press, 1996.

Fiorenza, Elisabeth Schussler. *Bread Not Stone: the Challenge of Feminist Biblical Interpretation*. Boston: Beacon Press, 1984.

_____. "A Feminist Critical Interpretation for Liberation: Martha and Mary: Luke 10:38-42," *Religion and Intellectual Life*. Volume 2, Winter, 1986, 21-25.

_____. *In Memory of Her: A Feminist Theological Reconstruction of Feminist Origins*. New York: Crossroads, 1983.

Gryson, Roger. *The Ministry of Women in the Early Church*. Collegeville, Minnesota: The Liturgical Press, 1976.

Harrington, Wilfrid. "Mark" (*New Testament Message*. W. Harrington and D. Senior, gen. eds.). Wilmington, Delaware: Michael Glazier, 1979.

Harrington, Daniel. "The Gospel According To Matthew" (*Collegeville Bible Commentary*, Dianne Bergant and Robert J. Karris, gen. eds.). Collegeville, Minnesota: The Liturgical Press, 1983.

Karris, Robert J. "Gospel of Luke" (*Read and Pray*. Robert J. Harris, gen. ed.). Chicago: Franciscan Herald Press, 1974.

*_____. *Invitation To Acts*. Garden City, New York: Image Books Publications, 1978.

_____. *Invitation To Luke.* Garden City, New York: Image Books Publications, 1977.

Kodell, Jerome. "The Gospel According To Luke" (*Collegeville Bible Commentary,* Dianne Bergant and Robert J. Karris, gen. eds.). Collegeville, Minnesota: The Liturgical Press, 1982.

LaVerdiere, Eugene A. *The Year of Luke.* Kansas City, Missouri: National Catholic Reporter, 1979.

_____. *Luke.* Wilmington, Delaware: Michael Glazier Publications, 1980.

*MacRae, George. *Invitation to John.* New York: Doubleday, 1978.

*Malherbe, Abraham. *Social Aspects of Early Christianity.* Philadelphia: Fortress Press, 1983.

*McPolin, James. "John." (*New Testament Message,* Wilfrid Harrington and Donald Senior, eds.). Wilmington, Delaware: Michael Glazier, 1979.

Meier, John P. "Matthew."(*New Testament Message,* Wilfrid Harrington and Donald Senior, eds.) Wilmington, Delaware: Michael Glazier, 1980.

*Nunnally-Cox, Janice. *Foremothers: Women of the Bible.* New York: Seabury Publications, 1981.

O'Collins, Gerald and Daniel Kendall. "Mary Magdalen as Major Witness to Jesus' Resurrection," *Theological Studies.* Volume 48, 1987, 631-646.

*Osiek, Carolyn. "Evolving Leadership Roles in the Early Church," *The Bible Today* 34:2, March, 1996, 72-76.

_____. *What Are They Saying About the Social Setting of the New Testament?* New York: Paulist Press, 1984.

Perkins, Pheme. *Ministering in the Pauline Churches.* New York: Paulist Press Publications, 1982.

Schneiders, Sandra. *Women and the Word.* New York: Paulist Press Publications, 1986.

Senior, Donald. "Gospel of St. Matthew." (*Read and Pray.* Robert J. Karris, gen. ed.) Chicago: Franciscan Herald Press, 1974.

*_____. *Invitation To Matthew.* Garden City, New York: Image Books, 1977.

*Stuhlmueller, Carroll. *Biblical Meditations For Advent and the Christmas Season.* New York: Paulist Press Publications, 1980.

*_____. *Biblical Meditations for the Easter Season.* New York: Paulist Press Publications, 1980.

*_____. *Biblical Meditations For Lent.* New York: Paulist Press Publications, 1980.

Throckmorton, Burton, ed. *Gospel Parallels*. USA: Thomas
    Nelson, Inc., 1979, 1992.
Trible, Phyllis. *God and the Rhetoric of Sexuality*. Philadelphia:
    Fortress Press, 1978.
_____. *Texts of Terror*. Philadelphia: Fortress Press:1984.
Van Linden, Philip. "The Gospel According To Mark" (*Collegeville
    Bible Commentary*, Robert J. Karris, gen. ed.). Collegeville,
    Minnesota: The Liturgical Press, 1983.
Winter, Miriam Therese. "Buried Treasures: Rediscovering
    Women's Roles in the Bible," *U.S. Catholic*. June, 1983, 6-13.
_____. *The Chronicles of Noah and Her Sisters: Genesis and
    Exodus According to Women*. New York: Crossroads, 1996.

BACKGROUND ON LITURGY AND RITUAL

*Campbell, Joseph with Bill Moyers. *The Power of Myth*. Edited by
    Betty Sue Flowers. USA: Apostrophe S Productions, 1988.
Emswiler, Sharon Neufer and Thomas Neufer Emswiler.
    Women & Worship. San Francisco: Harper & Row Publications,
    1984.
*Huck, Gabe. *Liturgy With Style and Grace*. Chicago: Liturgy
    Training Program, Archdiocese of Chicago, 1978.
Mitchell, Leonel L. *The Meaning of Ritual*. New York: Paulist Press
    Publications, 1977.
Procter-Smith, Marjorie. "Images of Women in the Lectionary."
    (*Women: Invisible in the Church and Theology*. E. Schussler
    Fiorenza and Mary Collins, eds.). Edinborough: T. & T. Clark,
    1985.
*Simcoe, Mary Ann, ed. *Parish Path through Advent and
    Christmastime*. Chicago: Liturgy Training Publications, 1983.
*_____. *Parish Path through Lent and Eastertime*. Chicago:
    Liturgy Training Publications, 1985.

WOMEN IN THEOLOGY, CHURCH AND SOCIETY

Burkhart, Walter, ed. *Woman: New Dimensions*. New York:
    Paulist Press Publications, 1975, 1977.
Coll, Regina. *Christianity and Feminism in Conversation*. Mystic,
    Connecticut: Twenty-Third Publications, 1994.
_____. *Women & Religion: A Reader for the Clergy*. New York:
    Paulist Press, 1982.

Fiorenza, Elisabeth Schussler. *Jesus: Miriam's Child, Sophia's Prophet*. New York: Continuum, 1994.

Gilligan, Carol. *In a Different Voice*. Cambridge and London: Harvard University Press, 1982.

Grant, Jacqueline. *White Women's Christ & Black Women's Jesus*. Atlanta: Scholars Press, 1989.

Isasi-Diaz and Yolanda Tarango. *Hispanic Women: Prophetic Voice in the Church*. San Francisco: Harper and Row, 1988.

Johnson, Elizabeth. "Images of the Historical Jesus in Catholic Christology," *The Living Light*. Volume 23, October, 1986, 47-66.

_____. *She Who Is: The Meaning of God in a Feminist Theological Discourse*. New York: Crossroads, 1992.

Kung, Hans and Jurgen Moltmann, eds. *Mary in the Churches*. New York: Seabury, 1983.

McFague, Sally. *METAPHORICAL THEOLOGY: Models of God in Religious Language*. Philadelphia: Fortress Press, 1982.

Oduyoe, Mercy A. *Daughters of Anowa: African Women and Patriarchy*. Maryknoll: Orbis Books, 1996.

Osiek, Carolyn. *Beyond Anger:On Being a Feminist in the Church*. New York: Paulist Press Publications, 1986.

Reuther, Rosemary Radford. *Sexism and Godtalk*. Boston: Beacon Press, 1973.

_____. Women-Church. San Francisco: Harper and Row, 1985.

Reuther, Rosemary Radford and Rosemary Skinner Keller, eds. *In Our Own Voices; Four Centuries of American Women's Religious Writing*. San Francisco: Harper and Row, 1996.

Schneiders, Sandra. "Effects of Women's Experience on Their Spirituality," *Spirituality Today*. Summer, 1983, 100-116.

Soelle, Dorothee. *Beyond Mere Obedience*. New York: Pilgrim Press, 1982.

Tamez, Elsa. "Guides Toward Reading the Bible from a Latin American Woman's Perspective," *With Passion and Compassion: Third World Women Doing Theology*, edited by Virginia Fabella and Mercy Amba Oduyoye. Maryknoll: Orbis, 1988.

Wahlberg, Rachel Conrad. *Jesus According To A Woman*. New York: Paulist Press, 1975.

RESOURCES FOR WORSHIP

Aldredge-Clanton. *Praying with Christ-Sophia*. Mystic, Connecticut: Twenty-Third Publications, 1996.

Gjerding, Iben and Katherine Kinnamon. *Women's Prayer Services*. Mystic, Connecticut: Twenty-Third Publications, 1987.

Johnson, Ann. *Miryam of Nazareth Woman of Strength and Wisdom.* Notre Dame, Indiana: Ave Maria Press, 1984.

Levin, Ronnie and Diann Neu. *A Seder of the Sisters of Sarah.* Silver Spring, Maryland: Women's Alliance for Theology, Ethics and Ritual, 1986.

National Sisters Vocation Conference Committee. *Woman's Song.* USA: National Sisters Vocation Conference, 1986.

Neu, Diann. *Women Church Celebrations: Feminist Liturgies for the Lenten Season.* Silver Spring, Maryland: Women's Alliance for Theology, Ethics and Ritual, 1985.

Neu, Diann, et al. *WomanSharing.* Cincinnati: St. Anthony Messenger Press, 1988.

Priests for Equality. *Inclusive Language Lectionaries (with Responsorial Psalms).* Hyattsville, Maryland: Priests for Equality, 1996.

_____. The Inclusive New Testament. Hyattsville, Maryland: Priests for Equality, 1994.

Riley, Maria. *In God's Image.* Kansas City, Missouri: Leaven Press, 1985.

_____. Wisdom Seeks Her Way. Washington, D.C.: Center of Concern, 1987.

*Walker, Barbara G. *Women's Rituals.* San Francisco: Harper & Row Publications, 1990.

Winter, Miriam Therese. *Woman Word.* New York: Crossroad Publishing Company, 1991.

MUSIC RESOURCES

Kirk, Martha Ann, with music by Colleen Fulmer. *Washerwoman God.* Albany, California: Loretto Spirituality Network.

Landry, Carey. "Are Not Our Hearts," in *High God.* Cincinnati: North American Liturgy Resources,1973.

McDade, Carolyn And Friends. *As We So Love: Song and Chants.* Wellfleet, Massachusetts: Carolyn McDade.

_____. Rain Upon the Dry Land. Plainville, Massachusetts: Womancenter at Plainville, 1984.

_____. Songs for Congregational Singing. Wellfleet, Massachusetts: Carolyn McDade.

_____. We Come With Our Voices. Plainville, Massachusetts: Womancenter at Plainville.

_____. This Tough Spun Web. Plainville, Massachusetts: Womancenter at Plainville, 1984.

Silvestro, Marsie. *In Avalon*. Cambridge, Massachusetts: Moonsong Productions, 1995.

_____. *Crossing the Lines*. Cambridge, Massachusetts: Moonsong Productions.

Winter, Miriam Therese. *Womansong*. Hartford, Connecticut: Medical Mission Sisters, 1987.

SCRIPTURAL AND SERVICE TEXTS

THE BIBLE Revised Standard Version. USA: Division of Christian Education of the National Council of Churches of Christ in the USA, 1973, 1980.

The JERUSALEM BIBLE Reader's Edition. Garden City, New York: Doubleday & Company, Inc., 1968.

Lectionary for Mass. Washington, D.C.: Confraternity of Christian Doctrine, 1970.

The New American Bible. Washington, D.C.: Confraternity of Christian Doctrine, 1970.

New Saint Joseph SUNDAY MISSAL. New York: Catholic Book Publishing Co., 1974.

The Biblical texts used in these pages are gender-inclusive and free adaptations by the author based on a combination of several English translations: Jerusalem, New American, and RSV.